BEYOND SURVIVAL

A Guide to Abundant Life
HOMESCHOOLING

DIANA WARING

Emerald Books

P.O. Box 635
Lynnwood, Washington 98046

Scripture quotations in this book are taken from:

The New King James Version (NKJV) Copyright © 1979, 1980, 1982 by Thomas Nelson, Inc., Publishers. Used by permission.

The Amplified Bible, Old Testament, Copyright © 1965 and 1987 by The Zondervan Corporation, and from The Amplified New Testament, Copyright © 1954, 1958, 1987, by the Lockman Foundation. Used by permission.

Beyond Survival
Copyright © 1996
Diana Waring

Published by Emerald Books
P.O. Box 635
Lynnwood, WA 98046

ISBN 1-883002-37-0

Printed in the United States of America.

To Bill,

The friendship we have shared for years has indeed

become the foundation for a lifetime of love.

&

To Isaac, Michael, and Melody,

the blessings and rewards of our friendship.

Acknowledgements

*T*here are a number of people I wish to publicly thank for their part in making this book a reality.

First are my wonderful parents, Jerry Gorrie and Joyce Bell. You have loved me for four decades—though, of course, you haven't aged at all! Thank you for always being there. I love you both!

Thank you to Phyllis Waring, my mother acquired through marriage. Your friendship, coffee, tea, and German chocolate cakes have helped get us through. What an incredibly precious gift you are to me.

Thank you to Edith Schaeffer, whose wonderful, vulnerable, insightful books changed the direction of my life and my family.

Many wonderful homeschool families have opened their hearts and homes to us, allowing us to become a part of them, to observe the dynamics of their home. Some must be mentioned by name: David and Shirley Quine, Bob and Tina Farewell, Tim and Bev Miller, Monte and Karey Swan, Josh and Cindy Wiggers, Steve and Jane Lambert, Todd and Becky Bishop, Don and Joan Veach, Jonathan and Alice Martin, David and Gerri Christian, Dan and Koleen Ingalls, Romeo and Lynette Delacruz, Ed and Cathy Green, Dan and Carol Matz, Bobby and Caroline Moore, Wendall and Rhea Perry, Lanny and Nancy Robins, Les and Carol Stadig, Ray and Holly Sheen, and Bruce and Barb West. Thank you all for your laughter and hospitality, the good food and great conversations, for being such good friends to "the wandering Warings"—we love you!

To Warren Walsh, Tom Bragg, and Jim Drake at YWAM Publishing and Emerald Books: THANKS! Your encouragement and support of this project have pumped energy into my veins—especially in the dead of winter!!!

My husband Bill is the unsung hero of this book. He is the one who has read and reread every word, editing as needed. His encouragements—"You can do it!" "It's not really *that* cold in the living room" (when it was minus 20 degrees outside!), and "Lighten up!"—have made all the difference in the world. His wisdom, humor, and grace make living the adventure of homeschooling a wonderful experience. Thank you, Bill.

Our children, Isaac, Michael, and Melody, have borne patiently with this process, cooking several more meals than the chore chart demanded! Their love, support, and laughter make our home a place I want to be. Thanks, kids!

Last, but certainly not least, is the One who has given me new life. Thank You, Jesus, for the strength, ability, and discipline to get up early every morning and write this book. You and I both know it would never have happened without Your prodding.

To the praise of the glory of Your grace!!

Foreword
Cathy Duffy

*I*n a presentation I make about teaching teenagers at home, I use two overhead transparencies to demonstrate what home schooling feels like for some teens and parents. One is a picture of a prisoner, because some homeschooled teens, feel like they are caged up at home and are missing out on "all the action"…like hanging out, playing peer pressure games, figuring out who likes whom, and all those other important socializing activities. The other transparency is of a mom. She's assumed the stance of a circus lion tamer, chair in one hand to ward off the attacking beast and whip in the other to get him to perform. It's amazing how many moms can relate to that one.

But homeschool doesn't have to be torture for the kids and a relentless struggle for control for mom. It can be so much more; it can be, as Diana Waring calls it, "abundant homeschooling." The trick is to figure out what makes for successful homeschooling and what doesn't. Unfortunately for those who like neatly packaged answers, but fortunately for those of an adventurous bent, the answer is different for every family, and sometimes for every child. At the heart of every successful homeschool is a vision that lends purpose to all our efforts—a purpose that transcends learning math tables and memorizing spelling lists. It must be a vision that spurs us on when the going gets tough and a vision that takes us to our knees to seek God's direction and wisdom. It must be a vision that parents can instill in their children so that homeschooling becomes a joint effort rather than a battle for control.

But some of us are short on vision and long on insecurity. Diana Waring happens to be of the "long on vision" type, and she generously takes our hand and guides us along her "vision development trail." I've gotten to know Diana over the years, more from her tapes and on the telephone than in person. Listening to her tapes from her *What in the World's Going On Here?* and *History Via the Scenic Route* seminars, I always came away inspired, encouraged, entertained, and a few steps farther along in the vision department. When I first saw *Beyond Survival – Abundant Homeschooling*, I was thrilled to see that she was finally putting some of her ideas down on paper for the benefit of those of us who are visual learners rather than auditory. But I was even more excited when I realized that this was not a rehash of what others have already said, but Diana's own, very personal guidebook for discovering the heart and soul of homeschooling. She takes us along on her journey, visiting with others who have traveled the trail before her, gleaning wisdom and inspiration from everyone she encounters. Instead of claiming the role of expert, Diana introduces us to the people and resources that inspired and directed her so that we can all share in the feast.

If you have never met Diana, you are in for a treat. You will definitely feel like you know her before you finish this book. One of the first things you'll discover is her sense of humor. I was reading the manuscript for this book on an airplane, and I had to keep clapping my hand over my mouth to keep from laughing too loudly and scaring the strangers who surrounded me.

You'll also discover that Diana lives in a very normal family, rather than one of those rare home school families that seems to operate in a totally different realm with nothing but super-achieving children, eager workers, and spiritual giants. Her husband Bill is actively involved in home schooling in a realistic way that capitalizes on both Diana's and Bill's talents.

This is realistic home schooling for real people! But it's more than that. It's an introduction to an adventure. So grab Diana's hand and hang on. I expect you'll be blessed and encouraged as you get to know my friend.

Table of Contents

Beyond Survival—
Abundant Homeschooling

*C*ongratulations! You are now entering an adventure guaranteed to change your family's life. Homeschooling not only changes children but also changes parents and even the dynamics of the family. As you embark on this remarkable journey, it helps considerably to bring along several guidebooks, maps, charts, and journals of those who've gone before. You're holding in your hands a guidebook to homeschooling as well as the journal of one family's trek on the "trail" of education.

Introduction

*T*here we were, poised on the brink of the jumping-off place. Much like those long-ago pioneers who prepared to leave civilization and head out in the wilderness to the promised land of Oregon, we felt like twentieth-century pioneers heading out into the wilds of homeschooling. We were bound for a better education, patriotic citizenship, Christian character, loving relationships, and a hunger-to-know environment. And much like our long-ago forefathers and mothers, we had those around us saying we were foolish, crazy, and too adventurous. We wondered whether we had what it took to make it through the Desert of Not-Knowing-How and the Mountain Ranges of Resistance, Failure, and Weariness. We heard of those who, unable to cope with the difficulties, had turned back, but we also heard wondrous tales of abundance and delight from others who had successfully negotiated the plains and the mountains and were even now living out our dreams.

We joined a sort of wagon train, complete with experienced wagon masters, to lead us to this new land. The experts' homeschooling seminars and books explained many of the details and difficulties of our impending journey and gave us some good tips for making our wagon secure, such as the reminder, "As for me and my house, we will serve the Lord" (Joshua 24:15) and the admonishment "Read out loud to your children." We covered our wagon with a canvas of family love, secured it with patient discipline, and greased the wheels with laughter.

We "sold the farm"—we did NOT sign up our oldest child for classes but ordered curriculum instead. We stocked up on provisions for the long trip—phonics puzzles, math manipulatives, crayons, playdough, desks, children's books, a library card—until our wagon was stuffed to the brim! With adventure burning bright in our hearts and a bit of fear and trepidation holding tight to our hands, we joined the other wagons heading out on the journey of a lifetime. We had no intention of returning.

This book is about the lessons we learned on our expedition: lessons in survival, some from the painful schoolmaster of experience, others from veteran travelers and guides along the way; lessons in protection of our children from the influences of today's culture; lessons in perseverance; lessons on living abundantly. It is also about the bountiful harvest we are beginning to reap in this new land as our children mature: articulate, interested, serving others, considerate, exuberant, creative, responsible—traits shared by many of the homeschool young people whom we find along our journey. It is, if you will, a homeschool traveler's journal and guide written to explain, instruct, and encourage you in your expedition.

Bill and I, usually accompanied by our children, Isaac, Michael, and Melody, have traveled across the nation for years, talking with homeschoolers at conventions, book fairs, and seminars. We have found those who are barely surviving by sheer determination and grit; others who are uninspired and bored but continue homeschooling in hopes that it will get better; still others who begin enthusiastically, doing every field trip and "extra credit" in sight, but find themselves wearing down or burning out; and then those who are having an abundant, joy-filled, exhilarating homeschool experience (yes, they really **do** exist!). We have compiled here many of the insights gained on our journey from each of these families as well as our own personal experience. As we've shared our hearts in seminars, conventions, and retreats, many of those attending have told us that our message encouraged them, helped them, and enriched their homeschool, even changed their lives. We pray that you, whether greenhorn or old hand, would also find that same encouragement, instruction, and inspiration in these pages and that you and your family will have joy in your journey.

*Jesus said, "I am come that they might have life, and that more **abundantly**"* (John 10:10).

Part One

☙

The Preparation

Chapter 1

⚓

Education Redefined

"Shirley," I begged, "what on earth did you use for curriculum when your children were little? I've never seen such bright, intelligent, eager young men as yours, and whatever they've got, I want for mine!" I had just met her 12- and 13-year-old sons, who were reading Tolstoy's *War and Peace*—for fun. My friend's sons had so impressed me that I waited breathlessly for Shirley's secret.

This homeschool mother of the most outstanding family I had ever met lowered her eyes, blushed gently, and drawled softly, "Well... they played with Legos a lot when they were young."

Our Journal

In 1987, starting our third year of homeschool, I came face to face with this question of "being educated." Our oldest child, Isaac, had begun kindergarten innocently enough. He had learned mathematics by stacking soup cans on the floor, experienced science by taking walks through the forest, and learned to read by reading books. He learned music by banging away on the rhythm set—you know the one Grandma gleefully gives him as she walks out the door to drive 200 miles away. Art consisted of creating sticky sculptures out of homemade playdough and displaying crayon masterpieces. Together Isaac and I learned about God as we read the Bible and prayed.

But now Isaac was entering second grade, and the pressure was on. What we did from now on would determine his success in life—and mine! I purchased textbooks and teacher's guides, borrowed readers, and received a free Scope and Sequence by listening to a sales pitch. My husband and I discovered a wonderful old-fashioned school desk at a garage sale for $10, and I even had an American flag small enough to fit on the desk. We were ready for "school" in the finest tradition—or so I thought. With great anticipation, both teacher and student began that first day of school with the pledge of allegiance, the rules of our school, and the school schedule.

It was all downhill from there. As we cracked the books, we discovered that our school was boring, irksome, tedious, and a drudgery. For the first thirty days of our school we endured the pain of filling in the blanks, matching this object to that beginning letter, looking at pictures of plants and animals so that we could answer the insipid questions, and counting striped balls on a page. As Isaac's curiosity began to wane and his resistance began to grow, I began to realize that I had made a terrible mistake! These were obviously the *wrong books*! Oh, no, what's a mother to do?? We'd already spent the wad for that year. I finally yielded to the realization that we would have to resort to the library, the zoo, and reading out loud.

Isaac had a wonderful year, but I suffered nagging thoughts about needing to get back to "real" school. Guilt gladly accompanied me to support group meetings and whispered my failures as other moms shared their successes. The apostle Paul's cry "O wretched man that I am" had nothing on me.

I told my husband, the professional teacher, that I was a washout as a homeschool mom and Isaac would be far better off in school. Bill gently persuaded me that this was not the case, and who better to know than a public school inmate (or was he one of the jailers?)? I took courage firmly by the throat and wrote out Student Learning Objectives (S.L.O.'s) for third grade.

As Isaac began third grade, our second child, Michael, a dedicated tree climber, was entering first grade. Melody, the red-head of the family, was four years old and just as determined as her hair color would indicate. She wanted to "do school" with her big brothers, regardless of Mom's best laid plans for mice and first and third graders.

And so began the Great Experiment. Could we learn—really learn—all together? Could I teach three children of different ages at the same time? Could children be truly educated while still maintaining the child-like wonder of discovery? Was this legitimate? And most important, would my children be helped or harmed in their education by Mom's experiment?

We began to try to bring in the creativity, to step outside the textbook. We began to experiment with reading poetry and children's classic literature to the whole family, to which they responded with great enthusiasm. We began to search for our understanding of what it meant to be educated, to try to determine whether our kids would be able to learn in this less traditional environment.

When it came right down to it, I didn't even know what being educated meant. My original assumption was that providing an education meant doing to my kids what had been done to me, but in a kinder and gentler way. You know, "fewer bells—better smells, more smiles—fewer trials." But as we muddled our way through homeschool for the first several years, that assumption showed itself to be based on a faulty foundation. For instance, filling out workbook pages, passing tests, and writing book reports do not guarantee that learning has occurred. We dabbled in this freer approach and found very encouraging results. Consequently, we began to search down to the very bedrock of what makes, and what does not make, an education.

So what does the word *education* mean? Like any detective hot on the trail of an elusive suspect, we began the deductive process: questioning the witnesses, following a paper trail, and applying the "little gray cells." The witnesses were other homeschool parents, our own experiences in school, and current graduates of the system. The paper trail took us to articles and books of all sorts: on education, on homeschooling, on learning styles, and even the dictionary. And the little gray cells? Well, let's see whether you come to the same conclusions we did.

The Witnesses

You've already met our first witness, Shirley. David and Shirley Quine, whose homeschool business Cornerstone Curriculum, Inc., made a tremendous impact on us, have nine children whom they have always homeschooled. Each child is "such a person!" as Patricia Polacco's title character in *Mrs. Katz and Tush* would say. It takes only a short time with this family to see that a superior education is taking place (evidenced by their reading *War and Peace* for fun.) When we met the Quine family in 1989, I was more than eager for an experienced mentor to help me negotiate the highways and byways of education. Who better than this successful homeschool mom and dad? So I became a sponge—soaking up as much of their essence and information as possible.

We learned, when we stayed in their home, that David and Shirley had a zest for introducing their children to the best, the greatest, and the deepest. Family times often consisted of reading great books out loud, listening to classical music, or gazing at art masterpieces. Math and science projects were hands on and fun and drew the children to think intuitively. Wonderful story tapes (*Your Story Hour*) abounded in the home. Fabulous discussions on all manner of topics regularly ping-ponged around the dinner table—fabulous because they were so free-flowing, interactive, and open-ended, a veritable forum of questions, answers, and ideas, with all welcome to participate. We saw the individualized care the couple offered even in the midst of such a large group. We saw how they involved outside sources for the particular interests of their children, such as ballet, piano, and government. We also saw that while they gave their children the opportunity and encouragement, they maintained a firm discipline.

They created such a rich environment for education that their children seemed to learn almost by osmosis. From David and Shirley we learned the importance of setting before our children an abundant feast of knowledge, sharing together each delightful morsel, and, in short, creating a wonderfully rich atmosphere for learning.

Our own experiences as children in an institutionalized school, the next witness, testified that the real learning—not the stuff you crammed into your brain just long enough to pass a test and then promptly forgot, but rather the material you still remember as an adult—took place only when we were interested. Teachers can create such an interest by creative enthusiasm for their subject. Bill had a fabulous learning experience in grammar, so that to this day he remembers elusive details, such as the need to place a comma after an appositive (whatever that is!). In college, I had the most fascinating professor for African history. All he did for one entire quarter was tell stories of Africa, and his stories were the spellbinding, sit-on-the-edge-of-your-chair-in-suspense type that you remember forever. My favorite French teacher (and the one who taught me the most) used to draw cartoon characters on the board to illustrate verb tenses—which I still remember because of the connection with his special illustrations.

This stands in direct contrast to the majority of our time spent in school, which we remember as an endless succession of unrelated forty-five minute boxes; as evenings spent cramming for the next day's test; as prisoners of the system waiting for the last bell to ring, the reprieve of summer, or the parole of graduation; as a sea filled with mediocre teachers and only a few bright spots on the horizon. I feel as though this time of learning should have been a foundation for the life to follow, but I remember hardly anything of my twelve-year sentence, and I was valedictorian of my class!

What do all of these experiences in school, the witness of our past, have in common? They suggest not that we need to become SUPER TEACHER, but that we need to work with the interest factor of our students. We need to find relevant ways of presenting the material so that it captivates our children, whether through use of a fascinating book or by storytelling, creating manipulatives for that hands-on experience, or showing such an interest ourselves that our students just want to tag along! There are many ways to present each lesson you come to. Later in this book, in the chapters on learning styles and teaching styles, we will lay out a few samples and, more importantly, explain how to recognize them yourself.

Next, we call on the present public school system as a "hostile" witness. A friend who works with suicide prevention in public schools, Mike Miller, says that if you've not been involved in a public school in the past five years you don't know what they're like—and you'd probably be shocked at what's going on. Since Bill has been a public school teacher for several years, we have had the opportunity to see current students of the system up close and personal. We have appreciated those who were alert and communicative, since so many, many students operate at a bare function of literacy. Too many students don't enjoy reading, don't know or care about the wonders of books. They can't, or won't, communicate deeply with adults, and among themselves they are quite limited in their vocabulary. S.A.T.'s have been simplified to allow for their inadequacies. Classroom crime has gone from gum to guns. Students know little about our country's history, geography, or biblical beginnings. They yearn to find acceptance in this hostile environment, look for love in all the wrong places, and hunger for self-worth in a king-of-the-mountain society. Many are labeled: dyslexic, ADD, ADHD, learning disabled, emotionally disabled, dysfunctional, and on and on. What they hear internally is, "stupid, worthless, hopeless, valueless."

Certainly, these young people need to be loved, nurtured, and introduced to the God of the universe who created them in His own image, pronouncing them worthy of His love and redemption, but—and this is the sixty-four-thousand-dollar question—do we need to send our own children into this environment as little change agents for God? Young children are unprepared for the war. As eight- or ten- or twelve-year-olds, they cannot absorb knowledge, stand up for what is right, AND protect their innocence, all at the same time. Then do we even need to duplicate those same educational systems, since they have failed in the schools? Do we really need to create school at home, complete with school desks, textbooks, 45-minute class periods, and recess, when we could have "homeschool" and spend a whole day reading *Captains Courageous* with breaks for hot chocolate and discussion? [Diana's maxim: If it's broke, don't model it!]

The Paper Trail

As we began examining the written evidence found in books—the veritable signposts of the trail—our definition of the word "education" expanded tremedously.

1) Have you ever picked up a book and suddenly found yourself at a meeting of the minds where the ink scarcely seems to be dry because the ideas are so pertinent to the question at hand? That's how I felt when I read *For the Children's Sake* by Susan Schaeffer Macaulay. Someone was expressing on paper what I had been secretly feeling all along—that children love to learn if they're taught from wondrous books, "living" books, books both children and adults enjoy. Usually, however, children are subjected to twaddle—the Dick and Jane type of stories—that no one would read if given half a chance. This held true for me, both in my own experiences as a student and as a mother/teacher of three children.

Susan describes her elementary-school daughters, in a very special English school, going bonkers (my word) over Shakespeare. No one had told the girls that Shakespeare was boring, hard to understand, and (as I once heard a high school English teacher remark) irrelevant. Instead, the girls were carefully introduced to the wonderful plots, action, and language of Shakespeare's plays by...*reading them!* In the process, they found the plays to be tremendously *exciting!*

This example illustrates the concept of reading very good books and learning from them, rather than solely studying dry and tedious textbooks. This has been lived out successfully in many, many families (including ours!). In Scripture we are told that "without a vision, the people perish" (Proverbs 29:18). *For the Children's Sake* gave me such a vision and a renewed hope for the possibilities of what our homeschool could be. In fact, I stopped worrying about our method of homeschooling, *sans* workbooks, and began to thoroughly enjoy, without guilt, reading aloud from wonderful books.

2)   An author I wish I'd met at the beginning of our homeschool was Ruth Beechick. Her homeschool books, *The Three R's* (for grades K–3) and *You CAN Teach Your Child Successfully* (for grades 4–8), were designed to walk parents through the seeming maze of teaching methods. Many parents say, "Oh, I could never teach my own children!", when what they mean is, "I don't know how it's done!" But Ruth Beechick's books make a straight path to the bottom line: the basic method of teaching.

A master teacher is one who tutors teachers in their craft, and Ruth is certainly a master teacher. As she tutors us in her books, she demystifies the teaching of phonics, reading, math, science, social sciences, language arts, and more. Her books simplify and explain the perplexities of teaching so that we are empowered as teachers to make decisions independent of textbooks.

I have a dear friend, Joan Veach, who would take her son's math book each year and go through it thoroughly. She would cross out roughly half the table of contents, explaining to me that Luke already knew this or he didn't need to know that yet. I was shocked—wasn't that sacrilege or something?—and puzzled—how did she know what to leave in?—and then, frankly, delighted—she was the master and not the slave to a textbook. Joan had training and experience as an elementary school teacher, which gave her both the courage and knowledge to make independent decisions. Ruth Beechick's books gave me that same basic foundation: an ability to teach without being dependent on textbooks. I'm not unique in that regard; many other moms have told me that Ruth's books did the same thing for them.

3)   One day Bill came home from a teacher training seminar with a stack of notes, tests, and information on learning styles. He enthusiastically sat me down to take the test to determine my learning style so that

we could compare results. It was mind-boggling to me to find that there are other people in the world who function similarly to me. I had always felt like the odd duck out in school. But, there on paper, was the proof that my ways were not so bizarre—there was a category for people like me! What tremendous freedom comes when you begin to understand the whys and wherefores of your children's individual behaviors! Bookworms are right at home in a bookish environment, but tree climbers don't sit at desks well, daydreamers don't complete workbooks on time, and cuddlers don't care what you know till they know that you care. As we began to apply this learning style information to our children, we began to understand why Michael was such a different child to teach than Isaac. And why Melody was altogether different from both of her brothers.

We began to understand why so many children are unable to succeed in an institutionalized setting. That it is not because of a child's deficit but because of a *difference*—one that even the best schools are unable to recognize, unprepared for, and unable to deal with. Schools are crowded. Pressed for time, teachers have to be inordinately concerned with classroom management, which doesn't leave much opportunity for individualized care.

Although we will spend an entire chapter on learning styles and another on teaching styles, since reading books about learning styles was part of our paper trail, we include it here. There are many good books on the subject, but a particular favorite of ours for homeschoolers is *Learning Styles and Tools*, published by Alta Vista. The book gives an excellent yet easy-to-understand explanation of four different learning styles. Included are tests to give your children that help to determine the patterns and habits that are dominant in their learning style.

You see, knowing the unique needs of each learning style adds a weighty defense for the tutorial system of educating. Tailoring your teaching to the individual child is a privilege not available in schools. It is what allows tree climbing, cuddling, daydreaming, and reading on an ongoing, daily basis, as needed, for your student to be successful.

God grant us the grace and wisdom to recognize,
prepare for, and deal with our own unique children.

4) A final signpost on our paper trail is the good old (and I mean *really old*) dictionary itself. Webster's Universal Dictionary and

Thesaurus defines education as "the process of learning and training; instruction as imparted in schools, colleges and universities..." My, how times and standards have changed! Way back in 1828, Noah Webster, the *original* American dictionary writer, had this to say about the word *education*:

> It is the bringing up, as of a child; instruction; formation of manners. Education comprehends all that series of instruction and discipline which is intended to enlighten the understanding, correct the temper, and form the manners and habits of youth and fit them for usefulness in their future station. To give children a good education in manners, arts and science is important. *To give them a religious education is indispensable* and an immense responsibility rests on parents and guardians who neglect these duties. [emphasis mine.]

An "immense responsibility" is right! All of a sudden, schooling takes on a much broader meaning—it becomes a *lifestyle* approach: not only teaching the three Rs but also teaching good manners, correcting the temper, forming good habits, and, most importantly, giving a religious (read "Christian") education. That describes a combination school of etiquette, basic training, and Bible school right in the midst of a grammar school!

Our experience has shown Webster's understanding to be pretty sound foundational advice. It is *valid* to take the time needed during school to address temper, habits, good manners, and more. It is not only valid but also *essential* to take significant time to give our children a true understanding of our faith (Deuteronomy 6). These concepts will be fleshed out in later chapters, but for now, suffice it to say that this 1828 dictionary definition is part of the paper trail. It leads to a much different understanding of what education is than the public school model we have received from our current culture.

The Little Gray Cells

Can you imagine raising children who couldn't wait for school, who had a zest for learning and the motivation to pursue knowledge on their own; children with a joy-filled, peaceful, and loving relationship with their parents AND their siblings; children who were quick to help others, articulate in communication, and earnestly established in their faith in God? This is not the impossible dream—we have been meeting families who are living it. Not perfect families, mind you, but homeschooling families who are living "abundantly." Not just a few families either, but several, and from coast to coast. The growing conclusion for us, drawn from the testimony of these witnesses and the evidence of the paper trail, was that educating our own children could be more of an adventure than we'd ever dreamed.

And so, we began to put into practice what we had learned in theory. We focused on creating a rich atmosphere for learning, where curiosity, questioning, and a hunger to know were encouraged rather than stifled. We sought ways of engaging our children's interest so that what they learned would lead to curiosity and more questions. The end result is learning that sticks rather than merely knowing answers for test questions that all seem to evaporate after the test. Storytelling, especially for history, became a favorite means of drawing our children in so that they yearned to know more. We basically threw away our clocks—no more scheduled 45-minute classes—and let animated discussions and creative output guide our class time. (One elementary school principal asked me what the hours of our school were. I answered him, "From first thing in the morning until we go to bed at night.")

Our children were encouraged to think independently: to ask questions; to compare and contrast differing points of view; to understand that the Bible is the final authority and that everything, **everything**, must be subject to it, and to understand why. We began to give first place and priority to teaching God's Word to our children, which impacted every area of our family life as we each grew in the "training and admonition of the Lord" (Ephesians 6:4). We began to read many books on the same subject to understand the differing worldviews that are promoted by different authors. Even our nine-year-old daughter asked questions about the "worldview" of her favorite children's author. We set before our children a cornucopia of living books for every subject and encouraged them to feast to their heart's content, while recognizing that they were learning and that valid education was taking place as they feasted. We studied "to present ourselves approved" (2 Timothy 2:15) in understanding the basics of teaching each subject area so that we were not slaves to a textbook, but rather were free to take what was useful, and discard the rest. Coming to an understanding of learning styles released us to do what some might consider weird things in order to teach each child effectively. (Example: Michael learned his math facts while doing jumping jacks.)

We change and flex occasionally as a better book or method comes along. We demand a lot of our children and require them to shore up their weak areas. Our children are willing to work on those areas, it seems, because we mix the hard with the fun, the strength with the weakness, the mundane with things they are curious or excited about. "Mom, I know I can survive today's grammar lesson because after that I get to do my next lesson in underwater demolition."

The results of this experiment? After nine years of homeschooling, we would never go back to "Egypt," we would never trade this experience of "excellence in education," and our children are growing to be more than we ever dreamed they could be.

Putting It Into Practice, or, Using Your Own Little Gray Cells

At this point, you may be saying, "Sounds great on paper, but how do I get there from here?" Or, "You just don't know *my* kids...*my* situation." So let's make this practical and personal for you. It will involve some homework on your part, plus some thought and discussion time. (Here's a hint, set aside time for a date with your spouse, or a day in a park for yourself, or something that will make this "homeschool homework" very special. Light a candle, or put on some foot-stompin' music, whatever it takes to get your creative juices flowing.)

Following are some questions for you to consider, discuss, think through, and pray about. As you begin to formulate your answers, be sure to **write them down** in a journal or homeschool notebook. These responses will be a lighthouse to you if you run into fog on your journey and an encouragement as you refer to them through the years. It has been amazing to me to look back at the questions we worked through several years ago and to see how answering these questions has helped guide us.

1) Consider your own schooling experience.

- ᨓ Was it good, bad, or indifferent?
- ᨓ What were the highlights, the best parts, the things you wish to duplicate? What made them so good?

∞ What were the worst parts, the parts you'd rather forget? Why?

∞ Do you remember much of what you were taught? Why or why not?

∞ Were there any outstanding teachers in your experience? If so, what was it that made them outstanding?

∞ Is there something about those teachers you could emulate in your homeschool?

∞ Do you see that your children are going to react in a similar manner to the things you enjoyed? To the things you despised?

2) Rate the atmosphere for learning in your home.

∞ Do you have good books on your shelves? Do you enjoy them?

∞ Are you a regular patron of the library?

∞ Do you have and listen to the best in music?

∞ Are there exciting stories available to read or to listen to about people in history?

∞ Is there a general excitement and anticipation in your home about learning new things? Not just the kids, but are Mom and Dad also trying new things?

∞ Does your family enjoy round-the-table discussions?

Even if this does not describe your current environment:

∞ Are you willing to begin moving in this direction as God enables you?

∞ What could you do *today* to make a beginning?

∞ What have you wanted to learn but had to put off? Could you try it now as a model of learning for your children?

∞ Do you have a support person to help suggest good books (whether purchased for your bookshelves or borrowed from the library), good music, good storybooks or tapes, and good topics for conversation? (This will have an effect on more than just your children—one of the benefits of homeschooling is the wonderful growth it produces in the parent.)

∞ Do you need to join a homeschooling support group?

3) If you have some experience homeschooling:

∞ What kind of model have you been following?

ᴓᴗᴓ Is it working for you, or is there dissatisfaction?

ᴓᴗᴓ Would you or your children describe your school as "abundant"? (If so, congratulations! If not, don't give up, there's help ahead.)

4) If you do *not* have experience homeschooling:

ᴓᴗᴓ Do you have a teaching model in mind?

ᴓᴗᴓ Can you articulate the reasons for choosing that particular model? (It's helpful to think about *why* we do *what* we do.)

ᴓᴗᴓ Are you homeschooling because of a "warm-fuzzies" desire to be with your children or a "grit-your-teeth" attempt to salvage their education, or something else?

ᴓᴗᴓ Do you see homeschooling as a long-term plan, or as a year-at-a-time plan with option to continue? (That will make a difference in your structure.)

Recommended Reading

For the Children's Sake by Susan Schaeffer Macaulay
> "Living" books rather than twaddle for a thriving homeschool. A wonderful book, regardless of your schooling choice. If I could read only one, this would be it.

Homeschooling for Excellence by David & Micki Colfax
> A family's adventure in homeschooling. Very interesting, thought-provoking book of a family lifestyle of learning. The authors sons have all ended up attending Harvard!

You CAN Teach Your Child Successfully (for grades 4–8)
The 3 R's (for grades K–3) , both by Ruth Beechick
> *The* manuals for understanding how to teach the various subjects—they put YOU in the driver's seat! I always tell folks that Ruth Beechick holds me by the hand as I homeschool using her books.

Dumbing Us Down by John Taylor Gatto, New York State Teacher of the Year
> An in-depth exposé of our current public school system by someone who should know. If a homeschooler

had written this book, there would have been a furious outcry, but coming from the inside ranks, it's all the more startling. It certainly adds combustible fuel to the homeschooling fire!

Cultural Literacy by E.D. Hirsch

Written to every American concerned about education, this book explores the concept that to communicate effectively, we all need to have a common base—a cultural literacy. This common base is taught through the great literature of the past, the stories of Western civilization, our beginnings as a nation, and more. Very helpful to homeschoolers especially.

Chapter 2

⟨∞⟩

The Blueprint

*A*ll the children were eagerly gathered around as Mom read out loud. You know how children are—always ready for a good story. Valerie Bendt, homeschooling mother, author, and all around super woman, was well aware that a good story can do a wonderful job of making learning exciting and interesting. For history, Valerie had chosen to read to her children a children's biography of Patrick Henry. Her audience was transported in time for a few brief moments to the American Revolution and the courageous colonists. Through all the critical moments of breathtaking action, the children were on the edge of their seats begging for more. At last, the final page was read, the book was closed, and they all heaved a sigh.

Curious to see what an American history textbook had to say about Patrick Henry, and wanting her children to understand the value in reading an entire book rather than two or three sentences about someone, Valerie pulled out a textbook and found the reference to Mr. Henry.

After she had read aloud the very brief mention given to this important historical figure, Valerie's young son complained, "Mom! They left out the best part!!"

Not certain what he was referring to, but happy that her attentive son had evidently learned something important from the biography, Valerie asked, "What was the best part?"

Imagine her surprise when, with a triumphant grin, her son exclaimed, "Patrick Henry didn't have to wear *shoes* until he was nine years old!!!"

Our Journal

Some years after we started homeschooling, I began to hear the term *unit studies* used to describe certain "wonderful" teaching experiences. I met people using *Konos* and others who had the *Weaver* curriculum, and they seemed to love what they were doing, although, to tell the truth, I couldn't understand just exactly what they *were* doing! Determined to not remain totally ignorant about something so wonderful, and since the Konos and Weaver booths were always crowded at homeschool conventions, I would stand off to one side of the booth, listening carefully, picking up bits and pieces of information on unit studies. From what I could hear, it sounded like lots of fun, made lots of sense, and required lots of organized work. Although I don't mind work, the amount of organizing seemed overwhelming. And I avoid structure like the plague. At that time, I didn't pursue these curriculums any further.

I didn't make much progress on the concept of "unit studies" until my friend Joan explained it to me. She drew some circles and lines on a board in the form similar to a Ferris wheel. Into the hub of the wheel she wrote the topic to study, for example, the moon. Then she began brainstorming all the possibilities of what could be studied having to do with

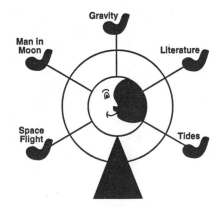

the moon and writing them in the capsules at the end of each spoke. Some of the suggestions were the man in the moon, literature involving the moon, the tides being caused by the gravitational pull of the moon, satellites, eclipses, phases of the moon, the origins of the moon, manned space flight and landing on the moon, gravity and what makes people weigh less on the moon. Each of these topics was then expanded and clarified with further details for study.

From the circle on literature, one could read science fiction (like C.S. Lewis's *Space Trilogy*), poetry, first-person accounts of space travel such as *Destination Moon*, and even young children's stories like *Good Night Moon*. From the circle on gravity, one could study Isaac Newton with his apple and Galileo dropping stuff from the Tower of Pisa. (Which falls faster—a pound of feathers or a pound of lead?) Each of the other circles on the wheel would also generate a list of topics and interests to pursue. All of these areas relate in some way to the topic "moon" and form the possibility of a unit study, making a natural connection between subject areas such as science, literature, history, and geography.

Joan was careful to explain to me that usually this wonderful, gratifying, stimulating, preparatory activity was done with her children. She would involve them in brainstorming the choices of what to study, of what was interesting to them, of what they would like to learn concerning a certain subject, etc. This would create a natural link between subjects (a unit study) and prepare an enthusiastic, ready-to-go group of students.

At last! The mystery of unit studies was unveiled! I felt like Ali Baba with all the treasure of the cave open before me. The possibility of studying knowledge that connected to other knowledge, which connected to still other knowledge, was breathtaking to one who had always instinctively rebelled against learning that was stuffed into boxes. I had loved English history and hated English literature, probably because no one had explained to me that they were intrinsically related. I had excelled in photography class but never bothered with studying the great masterpieces of art, because I chose to take one class and not the other, and no explanations of their relationship were given.

During college I was introduced to a new concept while viewing Dr. Francis Schaeffer's film *How Should We Then Live?*. For the first time, I saw that art, music, and literature were integrally related, creative expressions of worldviews and philosophies. Each is a portion of the big picture, the whole, rather than being isolated into little boxes labeled "no relationship to anything else." This means that art is no longer simply a subject to check off one's requirements for graduation. Rather, it is a window through which one can see history, ideas, philosophies, cultures, and more. Literature is not just a smattering of nice writings but is various expressions of the worldviews of its authors. The term *worldview* refers to a person's belief about the origin and meaning of life as expressed in the person's thoughts and behaviors.

I hungered to have the opportunity to relearn EVERYTHING from the perspective that these different pieces of knowledge are interrelated. This hunger had gradually gone to sleep after I left college, got married, had babies—until that day when Joan drew circles on a board for me. Then that hunger sprang up ravenously, exploding into a ferocious desire to see how everything related to everything else and to teach *my children* in that way. What a joy to have a chance to relearn all these things I never really knew and, more importantly, to understand their place in the scheme of things!

It literally changed our lives and our homeschool. Now a trip to the doctor for x-raying a broken finger turns into a long discussion of the science behind x-ray machines. Our visits to a local Chinese restaurant, owned by an expatriate of China, become the opportunity to learn first-hand what growing up in mainland China was like and how the architecture of the old-style houses protected and provided beauty for the women. A walk through an art museum in Duluth, Minnesota, gives birth to a new understanding of the changing worldviews from the Middle Ages to the twentieth century and of why our culture embraces hopelessness. A stroll through Mystic Sea Port in Connecticut is more than a trip through seafaring history. It's an opportunity to sing sea chanties, get recipes for codfish, be inspired to read Rudyard Kipling's *Captains Courageous*, and to learn the delightful habit of the Gloucester fishermen who have "mug up" rather than a coffee break.

Why a Blueprint?

The next three chapters consider teaching our children using the analogy of building a house. To build, we will need a blueprint, tools, and materials. Blueprints—what are they for, and why do we need them?

At one point in his life, Bill worked as an estimator for a brick mason near Portland, Oregon. He would carefully study the blueprints for a new house to determine how much brick was required and how much time was necessary to build the structures called for. Other contractors would study these same blueprints to bid plumbing, electrical, framing, sheetrocking, painting, cabinetry, landscaping, etc. Each of these individually skilled workers was required to turn someone's dream into a reality. The blueprints were the master plan for building a house, and in the same way, they are our plan for building an educational structure.

What do you suppose a house of today would look like if the owner did not use blueprints?

"Oh, I don't know, just build something nice, something like the other homes in this neighborhood...but, oh yes, my husband is 6 feet 6 inches tall, so make sure the ceilings are high enough...and, oh my, we have three children, so be sure to give us enough bedrooms...and, I almost forgot this *really* important, absolutely vital point—I just love cooking, so I have to have a HUGE kitchen with room for lots of appliances..."

Without a specific blueprint, can you imagine the potential for disaster? And dissatisfaction? And wasted efforts?

In the same way, it's essential to begin the building of our children's educational "house" with a blueprint, a specific plan, an educational philosophy. And just like in the previous example, since different people have different needs and desires, everyone's blueprint will be slightly different. Unless, of course, your children are "just average" and would be satisfied with a tract house, one that is *exactly* the same as thousands of homes around you. In our travels, we have yet to meet a single "average" child, so...on to crafting individualized educational blueprints!

I can hear some of you moaning, "But I'm no architect! I haven't studied for years to understand this stuff!! I'm not a teacher!!! I don't have a degree!!!!" That's okay. Consider this a crash course in educational architecture to get you started. Resources are listed at the end of the chapter to help you study this subject in more depth as needed.

Again, in our analogy, the blueprint is the educational approach you use in teaching your children. It is the format you use to present information. Since there are three different primary approaches—traditional, un-school, unit study—we'll lay them out smorgasbord style and let you choose what is best for your family. You may find it beneficial to adopt a variety of approaches, teaching some subjects using a different method than for others. You might find that you use a different approach for different children, and perhaps even change what you do for different times of the year.

The Basic House Plans

The first approach is traditional education, though followed at home. It involves having separate class periods for each subject, textbooks for each one, teacher's manuals, workbooks, tests, regular hours, summer vacation, etc. This is the approach we grew up with and are most comfortable telling others about. "What did Johnny get on his spelling test?" "He got 100% on his test this week." This is the most structured, most routine, and easiest to implement approach. Many states expect homeschoolers to follow this approach "religiously," you might say.

We have seen various degrees of the traditional approach used by homeschooling families, but the most *extreme* example is that of a mom we met on the East Coast. This mother had several children, ranging from elementary age to a daughter graduating from high school. The children's homeschool consisted of textbooks for each subject, for each grade, for each student. Each student sat at his or her own desk (as did Mom) and would work quietly through every subject. There was no deviation from the textbooks, no spontaneity, and a no-nonsense approach to completing the grade's work by the end of the year. Standardized tests were the standard of success. Strict hours were kept, and a rigid adherence to the textbook's pace was enforced. We could see, to our dismay, that some of these children were in rebellion, not only toward the rigid schoolwork but also to the unbending parents.

Families who appreciate greater structure will favor this approach to education, though seldom will they pursue it to the degree mentioned above. The pitfall to watch for is when the structure becomes the task master and the student is the cowering servant. We should instead make the structure a mere servant, so that it serves the student's needs and interests while we remain sensitive to the need for flexibility and spontaneity.

On the opposite end of the educational approach spectrum is what is known as unschooling. Unschooling involves little, if any, structure, no textbooks (unless requested by the child), and a child-directed pursuit of knowledge. In other words, unless or until the child wants to know something, it isn't taught. This approach works well at certain times for spontaneous, creative individuals who like to go with the flow. It utilizes the teachable moment—that time when a child really wants to know "Why do steel ships float?"; "Why do leaves turn yellow in the fall?"; "What makes a radio work?" This approach, however, is difficult to explain to school authorities, grandparents, and neighbors and can be impossible to quantify. "What did Johnny get on his spelling test?" "He doesn't take tests!"

We met an interesting homeschool father at a convention in Minnesota who displayed the extreme of this approach. As we conversed about the books in our display booth, I asked him about the kind of curriculum he used. He answered, "We don't use a curriculum." I assumed, then, that they elicited a hunger to know in their son by giving him a rich atmosphere of great books, music, art, etc. When I phrased this question, the man answered, "No, we don't do that either." At this point I could no longer hide my astonishment and asked him flat out, "Well, then, what DO you do?" "Nothing," was the careless reply. "We figure that when he wants to know something, he'll ask."

The obvious pitfall here is in not giving the child enough basic knowledge to spark any teachable moments. Enough information must be floating through your home so that the child realizes that there are things he doesn't know and so that he can form the questions you are so eagerly waiting to answer! As we'll see in the next chapter, *every* student needs to be well taught and well grounded in the three Rs if he or she is to learn anything worthwhile.

Somewhere between these two, and using the strong points of both, is the unit study approach. This approach can run the gamut from being very structured to being very flexible. There are unit study curriculums to purchase, or you can create your own. The method can be used with all the students together (multi-age classroom) or individually. Rather than culminating in a graded test, unit studies often result in a project that demonstrates what the student has learned. The approach can be described to those outside the homeschool community as integrated learning, or multi-disciplinary education. Since more and more schools are requiring teachers to interconnect subjects, this approach is readily understood among educators. "What did Johnny get on his spelling test?" "Well, he wrote a short story for publication, with all his words spelled correctly."

The most common concern parents have when considering unit studies is, "What if I leave something out?" That is a valid question and one that must be carefully examined. I believe that if a child is excited about and interested in what he or she is learning, valid education is taking place. If something is lacking in third grade, it can be learned in fourth or fifth grade as it is needed. However, if this idea scares you, simply find a good Scope and Sequence (for instance, *What Your Child Needs*

To Know When, by Robin Scarlata). Using this, plan out the areas that need to be covered in each subject for that grade, and then make sure your unit studies touch on each of these areas.

An increasing number of ready-made unit studies is available on the market, but one written by a precious friend is a good example. *5 In a Row,* by Jane Lambert, is designed to be used with children ages 4–9. The following description of this book will help to explain how unit studies, generally, can be organized.

Jane reviewed hundreds of children's books to choose the very best written, very best illustrated, and very best stories available. You read each story aloud for five days in a row; hence, the title. Ideally, you have all your little ones nestled against you on the couch as you read (warm-fuzzies opportunity!). After you finish reading the wonderful book, you talk with your children about different things relating to the story, which Jane has meticulously researched and written out for you. On Monday you might talk about some aspect of social studies (geography, history, cultures, traditions, etc.). On Tuesday, you might choose one of the language arts suggestions (learn about onomatopoeia, synonyms, verbs, etc.) On Wednesday perhaps you'll study the illustrations and practice making good art. On Thursday, there may be something about math to learn and practice. On Friday, you can explore the wondrous world of science.

These various subjects are all connected to each story listed in *5 In a Row* through an understandable, natural relationship. For your little ones, "school" can be completed in as little as one hour per day. Your

older children can pursue the subject areas for as long as Mom and the kids want to continue. From this, can you see how natural it is to relate different subject areas to a main topic? And how enjoyable "school" can be for even very young children?

In unit studies, it's as if we are spinning webs of wondering—reading books, asking questions, seeking the big picture—that we might catch the wonderful butterflies of knowledge and understanding. An amazing side benefit of this is that these webs of wondering make it easy to remember names, dates, and places that we might otherwise forget for lack of a cohesive framework. The bigger our webs become, the greater our knowledge, and the more we understand how it all relates.

Another way of expressing this is to picture our children's education as a house that is being built log upon log, precept upon precept, here a little, there a little. Each new bit of understanding science, each new discovery of a talent, each new comprehension of history, every increment of growth in communicating becomes the material that will be stacked one upon the other to create this house. As each child is unique, so each child's educational "house" will grow to be one of a kind. Some will prepare to follow in Michelangelo's footsteps, others will study to be a twentieth century J.S. Bach, still others will strive to follow J. Hudson Taylor. And that is only the beginning of the limitless possibilities!

Customizing Your Blueprint

Returning to the smorgasbord idea, it *is* possible to utilize all three approaches in your homeschool. Certain subjects like math, typing, and grammar lend themselves to traditional teaching with textbooks, class periods, and tests. You may be content to leave other subjects, such as economics, drivers ed, and drafting, until the time that your child shows an interest in learning them (the un-schooling approach). Still other subjects, like history, geography, literature, and science, fit naturally into the combined-learning of unit studies. You can also incorporate these different approaches to homeschooling at various times of the school year by choices in scheduling. And you may find that one approach works better for one year, while another approach is more appropriate the next year.

When my best friend from college days, Becky, was pregnant with her fifth child, she confided to me that the thought of teaching her two oldest during the months of delivery, nursing, and interrupted sleep was more than she could handle. Although she had always created an individual course of study for her children, at this point she decided to go with a "boxed" curriculum from the Calvert School. At the end of the year, she reported to me that her two oldest children had done extremely well, she had enjoyed the newborn days of her youngest, and she thought that she would do one more year of Calvert for her son. She is now back to her "regular" ways of teaching, but for those two years, the traditional approach made it possible for her children to continue their education at home.

Different schedules can be utilized to allow for different approaches. We've met families on our travels who follow a traditional approach for part of the year, intersperse it with occasional unit studies, and allow the summer to be a definite time of un-schooling. This kept "school" interesting and exciting for their children. One college I attended for a short time had two semesters of traditional schooling separated by a January term. The month of January was given to an immersion into a study where all other classes were suspended to let the students truly experience one subject area. It was such a wonderful break from the normal schedule that we would be quite refreshed and ready to resume in February.

My friend and mentor, Joan Veach, would tell new homeschool moms that December is a great month to put away the books and do unit studies. Since there is lots to do at home—baking cookies, crafting gingerbread houses, making presents, decorating the house, inviting friends over, cleaning the house for company—why not incorporate different aspects of this busy Christmas activity into your children's school and allow them to be totally involved in what takes place. Hold on to your hat while we take a quick spin through the possibilities!

⤫ When you make cookies, teach your children about fractions (the older children can practice multiplying and dividing fractions as you make triple batches of fudge or halve your aunt's favorite recipe of mincemeat). Sure, it takes a little longer to do that baking, but if it is also your schooling time, it's worth it!

⤫ Your children can study Caesar Augustus, the first Roman emperor. He was the one who decided to call for a census of the people in his empire, which required Joseph and Mary to travel from their home in Nazareth to Bethlehem. You know the marvelous, miraculous, redemptive result!

⤫ Your children can learn and practice the music of Christmas, whether on the piano, recorder, cello, trumpet, drums (!), or vocally. Then share your good cheer with your church or neighborhood.

⚬⚬ You can study economics as you check prices of goods before and after Christmas. If you make your own Christmas presents, have the children calculate the savings involved in creating homespun as opposed to ready-made. This would also be a great time to learn and practice percentages. Or you could teach your children this lesson the day after Christmas when the stores have those "75% off the lowest price marked" sales!

⚬⚬ The science of keeping a Christmas tree green for at least a month (our normal time) is an invaluable glimpse into biology!

⚬⚬ The scientific study of weather and the sometimes pseudoscientific study of forecasting is apropos during this time: "How reliable has our weather forecaster been this year? Will Grandma be able to safely drive to our house this week?"

⚬⚬ Chemistry experiments. I always unwittingly have chemistry experiments taking place in the back of my refrigerator, and we find these magnificent specimens when we make room for leftovers from our Christmas feast. (We don't really do chemistry experiments with them, although the whole family often gathers to comment upon what this or that might have been.) Actually, as my husband so generously points out, this is a lesson in both chemistry and economics!

This is really a short list compared to all that you can do with Christmas unit studies. I'm sure by now that you and your children can brainstorm several more related items your children would want to do for school.

Consider the importance of taking advantage of interrupted homeschool schedules to learn during unlooked-for opportunities. We have friends who unexpectedly had to travel from Washington state to the East Coast for business. Because of the nature of the husband's work, the family would be able to stay in the East for one month. They suspended all other studies for the rest of the month before the trip and concentrated on American history and geography. They read books, learned American folk songs, studied maps, and talked to experienced travelers about what were the must-see places. When the family began to travel, the children kept journals about what they were learning and delightedly collected all kinds of memorabilia. My friends and their children visited interesting museums, little-known historic sites, and Civil War battlefields in addition to other touristy interest points. And when they returned, it was with joy in having gained a greater understanding and appreciation of our country, and a definite growth in knowing America's history and geography. Not only was this a fabulous family excursion, it was a tremendous time of learning!

Even if you stay at home, this refreshing break can be used at the local level to pursue anything that promises interest and value for your students. Trips to a factory, a bee farm, a natural wonder, the local museum will teach lessons beyond any classroom setting.

This is only a tiny glimpse of the possibilities available to you in constructing a blueprint for your children's education. Since each family is unique in its needs and interests, your blueprint will probably be quite different from mine. I have yet to hear anyone, when walking into my home, say, "Oh, your house looks *exactly* like mine, down to the very color of your dishes!" However, I have heard people say, "Your couch has the same fabric as mine!" You see, we will have some similarities, but the very fact that we are unique, means that your child's educational structure will not be exactly the same as anyone else's. Your approach may be a lot like your best friend's, or it may be quite different. And you will probably need to alter your blueprints slightly from year to year. Ask any builder, who'll tell you that it happens *all the time!*

Remember, the purpose is not to live like the Joneses but to serve your family *specifically*. [Diana's maxim: If it ain't broke, don't fix it. If it ain't great, change it.]

Now, you're getting your blueprints in order, excitement is building as your children look at your "houseplans," and your house "site" is being prepared for construction (you're cleaning house, setting out home-school bookshelves, providing paper, pencils, watercolors, fabulous books, etc.). It's time to bring in the tools and materials and begin constructing your house.

Recommended Reading

Getting Started Books

Christian Home Educator's Curriculum Manual—Elementary Grades
Christian Home Educator's Curriculum Manual—Junior and Senior High
> both by Cathy Duffy
>> Cathy's books are among the most valuable home-schooling books on the market. Cathy has painstakingly

reviewed curriculums, books, educational games, and more to help you understand what's out there, what it's like, and who its audience is. An indispensable part of your homeschool bookshelf.

Big Book of Home Learning (Volumes 1–4) by Mary Pride

I remember when Mary's four books were able to fit into one book. My, how homeschool materials have multiplied! These books are your one-stop shopping place to be introduced to the almost limitless resources available to homeschoolers. If you want to know where to go to find the best foreign language programs or the easiest physics program or the Cadillac of reading programs, just ask Mary.

The Christian Home School by Gregg Harris

One of the most thought-provoking, insightful books on the reasons and rationale of homeschooling. Gregg's seminars, from which his book is derived, made a tremendous impact on us when we began homeschooling.

How to Homeschool: A Practical Approach by Gayle Graham

Gayle's book is a great tool for getting you ready to go. It was written to answer the beginning homeschooler's questions, since we all want to know about scheduling, setting up your home, organizing, keeping records, etc. Gayle's many years of experience both as a homeschooler and as a facilitator of homeschoolers shine through this very helpful book.

Learning in Spite of Labels by Joyce Herzog

Written especially for homeschool parents of children with learning disabilities, Joyce's wonderful book is a goldmine of truths about teaching for all of us. Very easy to read and understand. Highly recommended!

Unit Study Books and Curriculums

This is *not* an exhaustive list of unit study curriculums and books for the very simple reason that every year, more and more are written. This is, however, a place to get started. See your local homeschool supplier for more wonderful ideas.

How to Create Your Own Unit Study by Valerie Bendt
Valerie does a marvelous job of simplifying what seems to be an ominous task—creating your very own unit study. Based on literature, this book shows how to start with reading a great book and goes on with ideas on how to develop naturally related studies from that book. Very well written and easy to understand.

The Unit Study Idea Book by Valerie Bendt
If you aren't sure how to start doing unit studies, Valerie has compiled a book of 20 ready-made studies for you. Once you get your feet wet, it's much easier to learn to swim.

5 In a Row Volume 1
5 In a Row Volume 2
5 In a Row Volume 3 all by Jane Lambert
I only wish Jane had written these while my children were young enough to benefit from them! These books, along with Ruth Beechick's *The Three R's* and Susan Schaeffer Macaulay's *For the Children's Sake,* are my recommended package for beginning homeschoolers.

Far Above Rubies by Rebekah Coates, revised by Robin Scarlata
This is a wonderful unit study based on Proverbs 31 for high school girls. It is actually a four-year program that will amply prepare your daughters to be well-educated wives and mothers. The accompanying companion guide and lesson plan book are extremely helpful in using this program.

Listen My Son by Linda Bullock
>   Based on Proverbs 3, this is a four-year unit study for high school boys. Can you imagine the impact of teaching your young men all their studies from the basis of God's wisdom?

Alta Vista College Home School Curriculum by Alta Vista
>   This is a fabulous program using science as the basis for unit studies. There are courses on animals, plants, space, people, and more. Very detailed and very well laid out.

Traditional Approach Providers

Not to leave anyone out, I've included the list of those companies with traditional curriculums, most from a specifically Christian perspective. Please read up on these providers in Cathy Duffy's manuals and Mary Pride's big books. Then go to your local homeschool convention and carefully examine the companies you are interested in. You will save money and time and will avoid frustration.

A Beka

Bob Jones

Alpha Omega

Calvert

Christian Liberty Academy

Rod & Staff

SonLight Curriculum

Chapter 3

༒

The Tools

*A*s we pulled the mail out of our rural mailbox, we noticed a letter for our son Michael. Looking more closely at the letter, we saw that although Michael's name and address were clearly written, the return address was unintelligible. It looked something like this:

✳️◗▼❖◻️✳️✓✠∞✐✝
✗✜⁶⁶✦☆✿⇪✧
✐☖☞✚☆✳️⁶✳️☆★

With a puzzled look, we gave the letter to Michael, who eagerly opened it. "Oh, I get it!" he said. "This is from Alex, my friend in Maine. Wow! He wrote this whole letter in code. Sure hope he included the decoder!!"

What an amazing amount of time Alex must have spent creating and writing in this code! What will imaginative kids think of next? What a wonderfully inventive way to play with the art of communication—and to make sure your friends play it with you.

Painstakingly, Michael began the process of decoding the letter from his buddy. At first, it was a very awkward process, but as he became increasingly more familiar with the code, it became faster and easier. Eventually, the entire letter was decoded, and the happenings of the Delacruz family were shared with us all.

Two days later a mysterious letter was mailed to Maine from our house. Alex's name and address were clear and easy to read. But the return address looked something like this:

✶⁶✟❀✧✗⊠❧✶★
✶⊡✟★☞✿✠✦❀⁹
◯✈☊✶❧⊠⁹✶◯☞✿

Our Journal

Teaching a child to read seemed to me to be as difficult as learning Swahili. Oh, the mysteries that must be involved, the almost magical knowledge a teacher must possess! Knowing that this was my first great hurdle to jump if I was to continue homeschooling, I pored through catalogs describing the many reading/phonics programs available. Tightening our money belt, we laid out $250 for a method that even included recordings of English speakers pronouncing the ABCs! We waited in great anticipation for this magical material to arrive.

Isaac, who had been read to every day of his life, was five years old. When at long last the reading program, books, records, and games arrived, he eagerly sat on the floor beside me to look through the materials. My first experience in teaching reading began that very day as we had a phonics lesson that morning, a second lesson the following morning, and so on for the first two weeks.

During the third week, Isaac picked up an early reader's book and sat down on the couch. He spent quite a while looking at the book, occasionally asking me what certain words were. After about an hour, I asked him what he was doing. He answered, "Reading this book!" I smiled benevolently at this "grown-up" statement. My smile turned to amazement as Isaac calmly proceeded to read to me from this hitherto unread book.

After retrieving my jaw from the floor, I straightened my shoulders and gleefully thought, "Huh! Teaching reading isn't so hard after all." I'm sure God smiled at my naivete as He prepared for me lesson number two in teaching reading to my children.

Michael was born two years after Isaac, and from the moment of his birth he has been altogether different from his brother. When Michael was five years old, he was not in the least interested in learning to read. We had also read to Michael every day of his life, and he was content to let us continue this service, although his interests were in climbing trees, running, and wrestling with his dad.

I wasn't worried about Michael's lack of interest in reading, since I had read Dr. Raymond Moore's book *HomeGrown Kids* and knew that many boys were late starters. We continued to read to Michael, to Isaac, and to Melody, the three-year-old.

When Michael was six, my mother began asking whether he was reading yet. I calmly assured her that he was showing great progress in many areas of school, but his reading skill was not yet quite up to par. My mother gave me a slightly worried look and said, "OK."

The year Michael turned seven, he began asking Isaac to read to him, since I didn't spend nearly enough time reading aloud to satisfy his voracious appetite for books. Michael also began showing interest in learning phonics. I was sure that very, very soon I would be able to answer the grandmothers' questions about Michael and his reading.

Unfortunately, Michael's style was not the same as Isaac's. When Isaac was introduced to phonics, he made the connection to reading almost instantaneously. For Michael, it was a long, slow, uphill struggle that lasted for many years.

When Michael was eight, he laboriously worked through beginning readers, straining at every word. When we had a "poetry night" for our children, Isaac recited a long, funny poem, Melody had memorized a short, cute poem with my help, and Michael stumbled painfully through a two-stanza poem that he had chosen to read. That night I wondered what I was doing wrong and whether we were hurting Michael in his education.

The following year we moved from Washington to South Dakota which is described more fully in Chapter Eight. Bill had several opportunities to sit down during "school" and listen to Michael read. Bill shared with me how much Michael was trying but how little progress he was making. The pressure began to come in from all sides now about Michael and his reading. Suggestions were made of having him tested for such problems as learning disabilities and dyslexia.

We had, fortunately, just reread Ruth Beechick's little book on reading in which she describes that a student must pass through different stages to become proficient in reading. Some students jump quickly through the stages, like Isaac did. Other students remain for long periods of time in one stage and then move on to the next. We were able to analyze Michael's stage and realized that he was working on fluency in reading. So we put off all the tests for learning disabilities, thinking that that would only cause Michael more stress.

One day, Michael came to me in tears. "Mom, why can't I read yet?" was his pain-filled question. At that moment, God gave me an insight of encouragement. "Michael, Jesus knows just what you're going to need as you walk through your life. I think He is building strong muscles of perseverance as you continue to struggle to climb this mountain of reading. But you will reach the top, and you will have gained patient endurance through this time. Think of it like this—God is helping you to build your muscles"—and I flexed my biceps for him. (Not very impressive, but it was the best I could do.)

Michael's countenance brightened, he stood up a little straighter and gave me a great big smile. As he walked away, he had a confidence that God was walking with him and would see him through.

About two or three months after this conversation, Michael picked up a children's biography of Jim Thorpe. He was so interested to know more about this athlete that he asked each of us in turn if we would please read it to him. We were in the midst of getting ready to exhibit at a homeschool convention and had not a moment to spare. So Michael sat himself down next to a tree and began to read it. He was 10 years old, and this was the very first time he had, of his own accord, tried to read a book.

Bill and I kept a watchful eye on him that entire afternoon as Michael reclined against that tree firmly holding his book. We grew more and more amazed as he turned page after page after page, not coming up for air for hours. By the next day, Michael had finished the book and had started on another.

Since that day two and a half years ago, Michael has never been without something to read. He has tackled 300-page firsthand accounts of explorers, *Tales from Shakespeare*, books of World War II battles, *Robin Hood*, Mark Twain, and many others. This accomplishment, though it required a long, arduous struggle, has been very sweet for both Michael and me.

School Tools

What are tools for, and how do you develop skill in wielding them?

Picture #1: A carpenter drives up to the site of your new house in progress. He hops out of his shiny pickup truck, saunters around to the tailgate, and grabs a brand-new tool chest. You are *so* impressed as he manfully lugs the chest up to the site ("Gosh, he must be really good—look at all those...thing-a-ma-jigs!"). But your admiration soon turns to dismay as he picks up a hammer and mutters, "Hmmm.. now what's this thing-a-ma-jig for? Uhhh...ummm...hang on...I'm gettin' it...Oh yeah! I jus' remembered! This here's my holemaker!!" Your poignant lack of appreciation forces his hasty exit.

Picture #2: A plumber shows up at your nearly completed house. He gleefully reminds you that he charges by the hour and that his hourly rate is twice what you paid for Thanksgiving dinner! You show him to your now-to-be-installed sink and he correctly diagnoses the situation, "Gotta connect the pipes." So far, so good. But unfortunately, this workman is slower than molasses running uphill in December. He knows which tools to use, but he has no expertise in using them. And you are left to stew—crockpot-style—in your juices.

Picture #3: Your new house needs to be painted. You call Whirlwind Painting Extraordinaire, hoping they'll live up to their name and finish the house before your in-laws come for a visit. The painters drive up at the exact time promised. The two-man team works in perfect synchronization, with one covering windows and the other following closely behind with the sprayer. You stand and watch in amazement as this skillful team makes painting look like a ballet pas de deux. Every tool is used with extreme ease and skill, as if painting were as easy as child's play. With extreme gratitude, you willingly pay their "extraordinaire" wages. As they wave their white hats and drive off into the sunset, your in-laws caravan in. Thanks to the skill of those amazing painters, you're...uh... in the pink!

Now, which of these pictures would you prefer to represent your children? (That is a rhetorical question. Believe me, I already know your answer.) What tools are needed to build "educational houses," and how do we give our students the necessary skill and experience they need with these tools? How do they become "extraordinaire"?

In education, the tools of the trade are the three Rs: readin', 'ritin', and 'rithmetic. The ability to read accurately, adequately, and avidly is assuredly the single most important skill to acquire. Writing, whether by hand or on a keyboard, is the most important means of communication. Arithmetic as a daily tool is invaluable, whether you are a homemaker calculating the per-ounce cost of laundry detergent or a nuclear physicist determining, well, whatever nuclear physicists determine. Regardless of what career your child may choose, I'm sure you understand the importance of being skilled with these three "tools" that will be used day in and day out.

When we consider the three Rs as tools of the learning trade, it becomes easier to consider just what our strategy needs to be. Children need to be fully familiar with these tools, and they need to be skillful in wielding them. Readers need to be encouraged to read, writers need to have opportunities to write at whatever level of proficiency, and math work must be shown as relevant and interesting. Since each tool is important and necessary, all three need to be developed. (This was brought home vividly to me the year that my husband taught remedial math in a high school. The students had studied the same math concepts for years but continued to fail the course. As Bill worked with them, he saw that they understood how to do the math computations. What they could not do was *read* the problems. No matter how creatively or enthusiastically the math lessons were presented, the lack of skill in handling the reading tool made it impossible for those students to successfully complete their tasks in math. It also, unfortunately, condemned them to years of school time where they were considered, and considered themselves, to be "boneheads.")

If you have prereaders in your home, you must encourage a hunger to read by reading *to* them. If you have children who can read but don't enjoy it, that is, they'd rather take out the trash and clean the refrigerator than read a book, find a way to create the desire.

I recently met a wise mother with a junior-high age boy who had learned to hate reading during his time in a public school. When she decided to homeschool her son, she realized her most formidable task would be in trying to rekindle a hunger to read. Knowing that he had a passion for farm implements, she lured him into reading by putting a farming magazine on his desk. She then asked him to tell her something about one of the new tractors advertised in the magazine. As she told me about this incident, with a twinkle in her eye, she said, "You know, the striking color pictures all had captions below *that he had to read!*" It took only a few weeks of this kind of strategy before her son was caught—hook, line, and sinker. He began reading everything in the house having to do with farming. Wherever you live, whatever their interests, your students can be lured to good education through your strategic appeal to those interests. (If you can't imagine a teenage boy being hooked by farm implements, remember, this *IS* South Dakota!)

Children must also become comfortable as writers for the extremely important writing tool to be usable. The old adage "the pen is mightier than the sword" continues to prove its validity. (That's why I'm *writing* this book on homeschooling instead of standing at your door with a sword in my hand: "Ve haf vays uf maiking yu hom-schkuul!" You decide which is mightier!)

Although there are some who are "to the manor born" when it comes to writing and find it easy to turn out 300-page novels every week, all the rest of us *can* learn to communicate proficiently through the written word. I once heard a wise bit of advice about teaching children to write: Every day, have them write *something.* Whether they write the world's shortest short story, or Grandma's Christmas list, or a verse from the Scriptures, make sure they *write.* In time they will become familiar with this tool, and it is at that point that they can begin to become truly *skilled.*

To explain what I mean by skilled, let me share this illustration. A friend once told me about her husband's introduction to carpentry with a framing crew. As he told her about his first day on the job, he explained in astonishment that the workers could drive a nail all the way into the wood with ONE swing of the hammer! That is a wonderful skill to possess (saves lots of time). However, to attempt the one-swing method before you're ready could be disastrous. You could end up with a busted thumb, holes in the wall, and a nasty disposition! So it is with these educational tools—play with them first, learn slowly and methodically how to use them, and *then* work on developing the speed, finesse, and finely honed skills of a craftsman.

With regard to arithmetic, some have a natural math ability, and some don't. But everyone can learn addition, subtraction, multiplication, division, percentages, decimals, fractions, estimating, and negative numbers (particularly helpful when trying to understand the disaster in one's checkbook). Believe me, we bless our children for life when we help them become skilled in arithmetic, regardless of the moans and groans that may accompany the development of this skill.

Someone once suggested making a car game out of math facts. That way your children can practice speed and accuracy in a "nonthreatening" environment—if they're in the back seat, I can't threaten them! There are games, manipulatives, music tapes, and more to help your children gain the skill, yet we have found that they still have to have old-fashioned practice to firmly fasten math facts in their memory.

The skillful use of math facts will enable young entrepreneurs to calculate price of goods and net profit, which, if one wants to continue in business, is very important. We recently heard an illustration that shows just how important.

Two enterprising young men drove from South Dakota to Texas to buy watermelons. They purchased the watermelons for $1 each, and upon their return to South Dakota, they were pleased as punch when all of the watermelons quickly sold—for $1 apiece. After two weeks of fabulous sales, they were astounded to look at their company checkbook and to see that the finances were in the red. "How can this be? We're selling watermelons as fast as we get them!" With a little pondering, they came up with a surefire solution. "We'll get a bigger truck! We'll make lots more money, since we'll be able to haul lots more melons!" I guess they didn't have enough skill with the tools.

It is neither the purpose of this book nor my area of expertise to explain all the ins and outs of teaching the three Rs. Fortunately, there *are* some wonderful experts out there to help you. I suggest, again, for starters, Ruth Beechick's *The Three R's* and *You CAN Teach Your Child Successfully.* For teaching reading, we also highly recommend Wanda Sanseri's book *Teaching Reading at Home,* which explains what must be the Cadillac of reading programs, *The Writing Road to Reading.* My favorite book for writing is *Any Child Can Write* by Harvey S. Wiener. An invaluable resource as your child writes is *WriteSource 2000* by Sebranek, Meyer, and Kemper.

Many, many math programs are available to homeschoolers. One of the most popular is Saxon Math, which will take your students all the way to calculus, if they want to go that far. In our family we prefer Cornerstone Curriculum's *Making Math Meaningful* and *Principles from Patterns* (which is algebra). The reason for our preference is that David Quine, the author of Cornerstone Curriculum's books, wants children to understand the why behind the what of mathematics. Quine starts the children with blocks or graph paper or toothpicks to illustrate the math principle. Once the child fully understands what the principle means in real life, Quine moves on to the symbols and equations of math. This means that the abstract symbols are never divorced from the real world but, rather, are reinforced by it, even for algebra.

More sources are listed at the end of this chapter.

Scheduling Tool Practice

How do we take our children from raw apprentices to full-fledged craftsmen fully able to build their own educational houses? Let's consider the practical application of this analogy. How much time does it take for children to become familiar with these tools? What kind of schedule encourages development of the necessary dexterity and skill in wielding reading, writing, and arithmetic?

We need, first of all to understand the enormous task facing children who are just becoming familiar with the three Rs. Have you ever learned to use a new tool, even a new paintbrush or ice skates? Do you remember how the early stages of learning put a real strain on unused muscles, sometimes causing cramps?

When I was learning to crochet, my hands would ache after a short time because I was still training my fingers about what to do during the intricate weavings of the crochet hook. After a considerable number of practice sessions, I could crochet for hours without pain, and I really enjoyed the creative skill. As I've taught my children to crochet, I've had to patiently remind myself of the pain those early lessons produced.

In the same way, developing the skillful use of educational tools requires some strain and even some pain. Remember that as you schedule! Short sessions of initial practice are all a beginner can manage successfully before becoming discouraged, overwhelmed or frustrated. Short sessions of phonics, of holding a pencil, of adding 2+2 are recommended for the beginner and will be very productive over the long run. In fact, for the beginner, short practice times are far better than the long, drawn-out torture of answering *every* question in a section of a workbook. As children grow in their skills, it becomes easier and easier to spend more time wielding the tool. You will notice that your child is comfortable with all of the alphabet, can read beginner books, write his or her name and address, and count backwards from ten. Great! Now you can slowly increase the amount of time spent on this "tool practice."

The taking of a raw apprentice and turning him or her into a journeyman is a step-by-step, concept-upon-concept, lengthy process. As an example of this in the work world, when Bill was estimating for the brick mason, a young man was hired as a brick layer. The first day on the job, he looked at a trowel curiously, hesitantly picked it up and muttered, "uhhhh.... ummm...." The boss, realizing to his chagrin that this was not an experienced mason but a raw recruit, decided to take a chance. He patiently took the young man under his wing and explained just exactly what a trowel was for, how to lay mud on the block, how to use a level, and all the other knowledge needed for a beginning mason. Job by job, this young man developed mastery of the elementary skills and so was taught increasingly more complex skills. "This is the way to keep brick level over long stretches." "This is how you determine the cuts needed for a design." "This is where you start the arch over the window." It was certainly not an overnight accomplishment, nor was it "smooth troweling all the way," but after five years, the young man was a journeyman mason able to head up his own crew of brick layers.

Evaluate where your child currently is on the spectrum of tool-dexterity. Do you have beginners? Are they just beginning the process of *apprenticeship* in the tools of learning? Are they just starting to learn the first rules of phonics? Are you introducing them to numbers by singing, "1,2,3... Jesus loves me"? Is the sandbox your children's primary practice pad for writing A,B,C? Then bless them with a K.I.S.S.—Keep It Short, Sweetie!

On the other hand, are your students ready to become *journeymen*? Are they skilled and avid readers, with a book in each hand and one in each room? Are they showing signs of being a potential Pulitzer Prize winner for their writing? Do your children cover their walls with the mathematical computations for sending the next rocket to Mars? Then it's time to present them with some challenges. These students need a M.E.S.S.—Make 'Em Stretch, Sweetheart!

What, for the advancing student, are the possibilities for challenge? What are some ideas for stretching them past their comfort zone and into higher skills? Do you have students skilled in the basic use of their educational tools but who, again, need to develop toward their journeyman status? Here are a few suggestions we've come across in our travels.

READING: For the student who reads well, for whom it is not a problem to read for pleasure, it is possible to use the reading skill to open up a whole, big world of knowledge waiting to be explored. History records many instances of significant leaders who were self-taught through the judicious reading of books. The reading of living books allows the intrepid explorer to learn fascinating things about subjects normally relegated to textbooks. The adventurous reader can have a front-row seat at an enthralling historical event; experience the thrill of discovery as a scientist unveils a new bit of the wonder of God's universe; look behind the scenes of political manueverings, military coups, financial power plays, etc. The good reader, who has developed some mastery with this tool of reading, has at his fingertips these new opportunities that will at once increase his knowledge and refine his skills.

In our own home school, we have been encouraging our children to read the classics in literature. Since these books were all written before the time of short words and simple sentences, it has been a good challenge for them. This fall, Isaac, who is 14, was asked to read *The Scarlet Pimpernel* by Baroness Orczy and *A Tale of Two Cities* by Charles Dickens. He will be able to see the French Revolution from the eyes of two different authors and compare and contrast the two perspectives. Michael, age 12, began reading *King Arthur and the Knights of the Round Table* by Sir Thomas Malory and *A Connecticut Yankee in King Arthur's Court* by Mark Twain. He was looking for the contrasting viewpoints of the early Middle Ages from these two authors writing from different moments in history. Melody, our 10-year-old, wanted to read *Heidi*, so we included in her assignment another story of the Swiss Alps, *The Treasure of the Snow* by Patricia St. John. Reading different accounts of a specific locale gives a better understanding and wider exposure.

These readings will be illustrating the literary skill of the influential authors, presenting all of the challenges of higher quality literature. Along with that, though, will come an introduction to history and geography that will bridge into further, more structured pursuit of those areas.

WRITING: For those students who have learned some skills in writing, open the doors of opportunity for them to use those skills. Writing definitely improves with practice! And those skilled in communicating with the written word will have a *significant* impact on the world around them, whether it is through a ministry of writing encouraging notes to friends, or through writing letters to the editor about waning standards of right and wrong, or through writing a can't-quit-reading-till-you-finish novel about angelic intervention in human lives. Can you imagine the effect upon our culture if a whole legion of skilled Christian writers were mobilized? With the increased number of homeschoolers, I can cheerfully imagine it, and what is more, I intend to do my part in activating the mobilization of my own young writers.

These budding writers need to get their creative juices flowing and develop their finely-honed skills by being challenged. Have them enter writing contests, submit articles to magazines, write the family newsletter at Christmas, or compose a book of short stories. With the advent of desktop publishing, homeschoolers of today have tremendous opportunities to turn out wonderful brochures, letters, neighborhood magazines, and more. In fact, there is software out that will help guide a hopeful writer through just about every kind of writing that exists, including writing the next great American novel.

In our family we have several serial stories being composed weekly. We wait in great anticipation for the next issue of the "Jessie stories" that Melody so eloquently writes. Michael was captivated during a literature assignment with the idea of telling the story of Marco Polo through the eyes of his pet rabbit. Every writer knows the maxim "Write what you know." So, to write a good story, Michael is having to do a tremendous amount of research on this historical person and the places he traveled. Isaac prefers to hone his writing skills on letter writing to friends all over the country. It amazes me to watch him spend hours crafting humorous anecdotes of our family, just so he can get a guffaw in another state! But I'm sure it will all have been worth it when *Reader's Digest* sends him a check for some article, like "All in a Day's Work."

ARITHMETIC: Once a child has learned his math facts, it's time for him to begin putting them to use. We need to recognize the wisdom of the old saying "If you don't use it, you'll lose it!" So let's give our children many opportunities for practicing what they've learned and for developing speed and agility. These opportunities for using math are all around us:

- ᗡᗡ Good old math drills.
- ᗡᗡ Brand-new math games.
- ᗡᗡ Adding up the cost of a clothing trip as Dad's arms fill up.
- ᗡᗡ Computing the best values in a grocery store on a per-ounce basis.
- ᗡᗡ Determining how many miles are left on this tank of gas—before you run out.
- ᗡᗡ Figuring the realistic budget of your upcoming vacation, including T-shirts and bumperstickers.

A wonderful, must-read book that illustrates this point in real life is *Carry On, Mr. Bowditch*. It is the captivating true story of Nathaniel Bowditch of Salem, Massachusetts. Nathaniel loved "figuring" and kept challenging himself to new mathematical heights. As he grew to manhood, this skill made him invaluable to sea captains who needed good bookkeepers. On board ship, Nathaniel developed a reliable means for calculating the ship's location based on star sightings, which was a godsend to the pilots. Even more amazingly, he taught the technique to every sailor on board! Later in life, he took on the massive task of refiguring the faulty navigational tables of his time, perhaps his greatest achievement. Each step of the way, in Nathaniel Bowditch's life was preparation for the next step, and each skill learned enabled him to develop increasingly more difficult math skills for his occupation.

In our home, math has been both a blessing and a curse. As we grow and develop skill in handling our finances, we are blessed. When we neglect to take into account interest rates, negative numbers, and declining values, we have been both cursed and very close to cursing! You may have already guessed that budgeting is not one of my strong suits. However, as my children learned about money management, economics, and the mathematical value of earning interest, they wanted to help me develop some "overcomer" tendencies in that area. So they presented me with several envelopes, marked with appropriate categories, in which to keep my budgeted money. My own children have, in some areas, learned exceedingly well and have become MY teacher, to help me grow and develop. Allow your children to use their developing math skills in the everyday life of your family, and watch what happens!

All right. You've gathered up your "tool manuals," evaluated where your children are on the "tool-usability spectrum," and set an appropriate schedule for their growing development. Congratulations! Now you're ready to begin building! But, you may ask, what are the materials we are going to use to build? I've yet to see a house *constructed* of hammers, saws, and screwdrivers, though these tools are certainly used in the construction process. Houses are made of various kinds of materials—brick, wood, glass, cement, steel, stone—and these materials are the "stuff" used in creating unique, individual houses. The next chapter examines the brick, the wood, and the glass of an educational house.

Recommended Reading

The 3 R's by Ruth Beechick
You CAN Teach Your Child Successfully by Ruth Beechick
    The manuals for understanding how to teach the various subjects—they put YOU in the driver's seat! I always tell folks that Ruth Beechick holds me by the hand as I homeschool using her books.

Teaching Reading at Home by Wanda Sanseri
    My absolute favorite program for developing readers, spellers, and writers. It makes sense of *The Writing Road to Reading* by Ramalda Spaulding and is an invaluable tool for presenting the wonderful, systematic teaching of the English language. I finally understand why we spell school with a "ch."

Alpha Phonics by Samuel Blumenfeld
    We used this very helpful phonics program with Michael in his last year before reading. I am convinced that Mr. Blumenfeld's presentation was part of the reason that Michael gained confidence to read.

Any Child Can Write by Harvey S. Weiner
    Again, my favorite book describing the very messy process of writing something worth writing. I think it is a must have.

Writesource 2000 by Sebranek, Meyer, and Kemper
    The one writing resource that you need. I can never remember which comes first in a business letter, the date or the other person's address. This is the book that will tell you!

Learning Language Arts Through Literature, Common Sense Publishing
    This age-graded series uses excerpts from good books for the basis of the students' lessons. The parts of speech, punctuation, etc., are highlighted as they appear within the excerpts. The students read, write, copy, analyze, and imitate work by the best authors to create language art lessons.

Easy Grammar by Wanda Phillips

I am not the one to teach grammar in our house—I never studied it until I took French in college! So Bill teaches the grammar lessons, and this is one of his most-often used sources. It is thorough, no-nonsense, tried and true.

Simply Grammar by Charlotte Mason, edited by Karen Andreola

This presents a wonderful concept in teaching grammar. Rather than filling out never-ending blanks in a grammar book, *Simply Grammar* leads the students along verbally. You and your children look at pictures and discuss the nouns that you see or the verbs that are being done, etc. It DOES help to know some grammar before using this to teach your children. Bill has used it extensively in our homeschool to complement *Easy Grammar*.

Understanding Writing by Susan Braderick

Based on the book, *Any Child Can Write*, this is a K–12 language arts program written from a Christian perspective. Braderick has done a wonderful job of structuring the many ideas Wiener suggested. It is all laid out in specific detail for your ease of use.

Writing Strands by National Writing Institute

A wonderful creative writing course, this is an age-graded program. Is it effective? Yes! It puts writing "in the blood" and helps to develop your budding Pulitzer Prize winners.

Making Math Meaningful by David Quine
Principles from Patterns by David Quine

Cornerstone Curriculum's age-graded math programs are our favorites. Math becomes far more than just filling in the blank and getting the right answer. The student learns the whys and wherefores of mathematics. Quine includes clear explanations, puzzles, and drills, etc. The lessons are scripted so that you, as the teacher, know what to ask and how your students should respond.

Saxon Math by John Saxon and Stephen Hake
   If you're looking for a traditional textbook approach for math, this is the most popular one among home-schoolers.

Chapter 4

⟡

The Materials

*A*t first glance they looked like an ordinary homeschool family: happy, hospitable, gracious, interested, and interesting. But, as we soon discovered, there was much more to Chris and Allan Miller than first met the eye. Their mom, Bev, took us into the converted garage that now housed her husband Tim's at-home engineering business. Standing on the other side of the room from Tim's computer desk was an enormous drafting table, and framed pictures of Mickey Mouse decorated the walls. Well-used books of cartooning, animating, and the making of Disney feature films rested upon adjacent shelves. And covering every square inch of the table itself were intriguing hand-drawn cartoons. Bev explained to us that her teenage sons were in the process of creating an animated video as part of their homeschool work. Chris and Allan then explained to us the step-by-step process used to animate on film and how much still remained to complete their project.

Struggling to pick my tongue up off the floor, I said something intelligent, like, "Wow!" To begin with, I had thought animating cartoons was just a matter a drawing some pictures and putting them together (kind of like an advanced flip book). The reality of all the work involved was staggering! In addition, I wondered how on earth these two young men had learned all this stuff. There was not a single professional animator in sight. Finally, the Miller family seemed as normal as we are. Was it possible for normal homeschool students to produce an animated video without having parents in the "biz," not to mention *not* having all the high-tech equipment professionals use? The answer was sitting articulately on the drawing table.

Our Journal

Sometime during the early years of our homeschooling, I heard about a new "discovery" in psychology called the seven intelligences. The person who enthusiastically described this new wonder of the academic world said, "This shows that *all* children are gifted, not just the few we've been acknowledging. It's simply a matter of recognizing the area where each child's gifting resides."

It was nice to hear confirmed what we had known all along: that our children were each created by God with specific abilities and interests. I was coming to understand that these abilities were given in anticipation of what God had for them to accomplish in their lives. As a result, we began making room for their differences, their interests, and their abilities in our homeschool schedule. This is the way it shaped up for our son Isaac.

Isaac has always shown a remarkable affinity for music. When he was about five months old, we noticed him bouncing in time to the tape we were listening to—Gaelic music with a very specific rhythmic beat. When he went to the pediatrician's office for his two-year-old checkup, Isaac astounded the good doctor by singing the ABC song *on pitch*! When he was four, he could pick out children's songs on the piano—by ear. He could remember songs he'd heard only once and was constantly amazing us with new musical feats. Isaac began studying piano with a wonderful teacher who both challenged him and allowed him to experiment with his musical ideas.

Three years ago, we began touring the nation doing a concert of American historic folk music, and conducting seminars for homeschooling parents. The concert was based on the *History Alive! Through Music* series (described further in Chapter Five) that I had written. Isaac kept asking if he could sing with me on stage. With a little fear and trepidation, we added all three children to the concert. Dressed in historic costumes, they sang and performed skits while I sang the songs and told the stories of America.

What an incredible boost and encouragement it was to have all three children on stage, but especially to have Isaac's wonderful harmonies belting out with my melodies. It has certainly been worth the time to practice together, to work out parts together, and to grow musically together.

This fall, Isaac asked if he could play the conga drum with our church's worship team. I know that I should stop being amazed at his musical dexterity, but I nearly fell over in shock during his first rehearsal. He played those drums like a pro, though he's never had a lesson and had practiced for only two days.

In his most recent endeavor, Isaac picked up my guitar, intending to begin learning it for his music assignment in school. That was fine with me, sort of a "chip off the old block." What was unique to Isaac's experience, however, was that he started to figure out the chords without any help and without any music. Nevertheless, about a half hour later, he walked out and displayed the three chords he knew. (Never in my wildest dreams would I have attempted that!!!)

When it comes to music, we allow Isaac a lot of leeway to try things, to experiment, to practice. Because of the obvious gifting in his life, we believe this is one of the major materials we are using to build Isaac's educational house.

Material Matters

What materials do people use to build houses? What materials do we use to build educational houses?

Material #1. I have always had a secret yen to own a log home. There is something so cozy and warm about log cabins, something that just makes me want to curl up with a good book and a cup of cocoa. Each log home I've been in or seen in magazines has had such an individual personality that it seems to me that they are close to being alive. I suppose that comes from being made from cut-down living trees!

Material #2. The brick mason Bill used to work for, Larry Bonife, and his wife Brenda built their first home out of brick. That was not surprising at all. What did surprise me, however, was entering their home for the first time and seeing *interior* walls made out of brick! It seemed a highly appropriate home for a brick mason, but I must admit, you really have to like brick a lot to have it in your bedroom. Larry and Brenda's home was one of a kind and was highly sought by brick lovers when they put it up for sale.

Material #3. My mother lives on a picturesque lake. Directly across the water is a snow-covered majestic mountain that seems to rise up spectacularly as a lofty sentinel over the lake. When my mother made her house plans, she specified that the wall facing the mountain and lake was to be all glass. And so it is. From the peak of the 15-foot ceiling to the rug-covered floor, the wall is made entirely of glass, with just a wooden framework to hold it in place. Her entire magnificent house was planned around this glass wall and the view it revealed.

Material #4. When I was growing up in Miami, Florida, we lived in a concrete house. It was painted a pretty color, but it was still concrete. There was not a piece of wood siding in sight in my whole neighborhood. Do you know why? While we lived in that house, we survived three tremendous hurricanes, and our house was undamaged. One neighbor had a wooden roof over his deck, but that was swept away during one of the hurricanes. Wood is just not a stable commodity during a hurricane. Lest you begin to feel sorry for me (unless you live in Florida and know about these things), let me hasten to add that we had our very own *cement* in-ground swimming pool. So we actually enjoyed living in that concrete house. (I used to beg my parents to let me have my own porpoise, like Flipper.)

All of these houses were just houses. But each house that I've described is very different, made unique by both the blueprint chosen and the materials used to construct it. A house built from logs will have a different feel to it from a house made of brick. And a house made of glass will be entirely different from a house composed of concrete block. You may simply drool over the thought of living in one and abhor the very notion of living in another. That's great! You see, it would be very boring if we all were required to live in houses that were exactly the same.

(Actually, Bill once applied for a teaching job in a small town on the plains of the Midwest. We knew something was wrong as we drove into the town for the interview but couldn't put our finger on it. As we drove up and down the streets looking for the school, we suddenly realized that every single house we had passed was *white*. Every single one! And the houses all looked basically the same from the outside. Now, I really enjoy white as the main color of a house, but *all* of these houses were white, ALL white. Thankfully, Bill was not chosen for that position, or else I might have ended up in a *white* coat—straitjacket version!)

It is a tremendous blessing from God that we have such different tastes. It is also a tremendous blessing that He's gifted all of us in such different ways. What astounds me is that He's created so much for us to learn about, so many areas of interests, so many subjects to study. (Have you ever thought about the almost infinite number of different types of bugs? And all of the people who have made it their life's work to catalog them?!) I think God really enjoys variety!

In this analogy, the materials used to build our educational houses are those many, varied areas of interest, such as history, science, music, art, geography, technology, and economics. The fascinating world of interpersonal relationships, foreign cultures, missions, evangelism, political systems, communications, and military strategies shows what diversity there is in the spheres of knowledge.

Consider this: What is vital in equipping someone to build wells in Somalia under the auspices of a missionary society is quite different from the background one needs to work at Mission Control, Houston. Someone who is gifted in communications will have different study interests from the student planning to research a new, soil-friendly fertilizer. What a fantastic prospect! We are all different, with different interests, careers, and passions to pursue.

Have you ever heard the scientific analysis that there are no two snowflakes alike? (I've always wondered how they knew that, since I've yet to see a lab-coated scientists in my front yard looking at the Waring family's snowflakes under a microscope.) If this is true about snowflakes, how much more do you suppose that God has created each one of us unique and individual? No two of us in the whole world alike—what a wonderful thing to contemplate. That means that when God made us, He did, in fact, throw away the mold. So then, why do we try to shoehorn our children into studying *exactly* the same subjects, in the same way, in the same scope and sequence as a school or anyone else? Is there a better way to do this, one that takes into account our God-given direction, interests, and talents?

As we look back in history, this shoehorning is seldom evident in the lives of famous people. In studying some of these people who were so greatly influential in politics, wars, missions, art, etc., it has been very revealing to see how their childhood bents were encouraged and developed. Frequently, we observe how that bent shaped the future of the adult.

George Washington Carver, the remarkable scientist who, among other things, discovered the value of growing peanuts, started his life as a sickly slave boy during the Civil War. Because he was not strong enough to work in the fields, he was allowed to do odd jobs at the house, which left him free to wander in the woods much of the time. George began observing plants in their natural settings, then started experimenting with ways to encourage ailing plants. Soon he was known around the area as the person to see when your plants needed help, sort of our first plant doctor. He even had an infirmary for these sickly plants out in the woods. After the war, he started his formal education, advancing up through college studies. And to no one's surprise, his field of study was botany. (If you don't know the rest of the story, it's worth a quick trip to the library to "Read More About It.")

George Frideric Handel had the gift of God for creating wonderful music. His father had intended him to study law, but when a duke heard George playing the special music for a church service, all that changed. He was only about eight years old when he was "discovered," and he began formally studying music at that very early age. I don't know about you, but every time I sing the "Hallelujah Chorus" from Handel's *Messiah*, I am thankful that his talents were given the training to flourish.

On a more earth-shaking note, Alexander the Great started life as the son of a Macedonian king who was preparing the armies of Greece to fight Persia. Alexander studied Greek culture and knowledge under Aristotle and absorbed intriguing strategies of war from his father, King Philip. In fact, as a boy, he was so absorbed with anticipation of conquest that he is said to have lamented that his father would get ahead of him and would leave Alexander nothing to do! When his father was assassinated, Alexander, at age 20, was more than ready to step into his father's shoes. Taking the well-prepared army, he fashioned it into the leanest, meanest fighting machine the world has ever known. In just thirteen short years, Alexander the Great and his army conquered the *entire known world*. In so doing, Alexander had the golden opportunity to spread the Greek culture and language throughout his empire.

Do you see, God had His hand moving sovereignly through all of this. Because of Alexander's domination of the surrounding cultures, Greek became the common trade language. Three hundred years later, having this common language allowed the gospel message to spread like wildfire throughout the world. Doesn't that just make you want to shout? God even gifts military strategists!

These are but a few examples from history of the amazing ways that childhood bents develop into lifelong pursuits. When you translate that concept into our analogy, you see that a house could be constructed almost entirely of only one material, such as brick, wood, or glass, yet for that house, the material would look completely appropriate.

For our children, we see much the same dynamic in their bents. Some children are born to be artists (you can easily tell—they walk around the house wearing berets.). Others are obviously scientist-inventors (they are the ones who take apart all of your gadgets, then put them back together better than before.). Some children are born to dazzle with their God-given musical talents. Others hold us spellbound with their ability to spin tales. Some children are "deluxe combos"—they love studying history, creating cartoon art, and fiddling with computers. Perhaps God's gifting in them is to be an effective, righteous political cartoonist. In God's economy, each of us has something especially unique to do. So He gifts us with a unique blend of interests, talents, and hungers to know.

These students who demonstrate such an interest should be allowed to go further in their pursuits, given extra time, extra opportunity. Now, not every child will wish to commit to the arduous effort it takes to excel. Not all children, at least not all at the same time, display a passion for a lifelong pursuit. But for a Handel, a Michelangelo, or a Carver, don't be afraid to allow them the latitude to pursue their giftings.

Just as you can build a house of bricks or logs or glass, so too can you build a house incorporating bricks *and* logs *and* glass. In fact, it is much more common to construct a house with a number of different materials than it is to build a house using a single material. Even houses of brick have windows of glass and wooden doors. Log houses may have steel sinks and brick fireplaces. Glass houses can utilize wooden frames and stone flooring.

Just as the skillful blending of diverse materials provides individuality to your house, in the same way, your children will need a sampling of many different subject materials to build their educational houses, whether or not they are displaying a passion in a certain field. A sampling, however, does not mean an exhaustive knowledge of each area; it means a sampling: a touch of this, a bit of that, a taste of this, a whiff of that, until they have received a broad and thorough foundation.

A sampling of subjects is called a "minimum proficiency" in all the main areas of knowledge. This means that every student should have at least a minimum proficiency in history, science, literature, economics, art, music, and the Bible. This could include an overview of world and American history, an understanding of the basic scientific systems, a good exposure to the classics and other great literature, a realistic comprehension of supply and demand, an appreciation of art and a developed taste for classical music, and a systematic understanding of theology. For flexibility in later life, our children should know something about how to cook, sew, build, repair, change a tire, and garden (these are considered life skills).

Whether they make gourmet cooking their major occupation or merely know enough to make biscuits from scratch is up to their unique interests. Whether they write best-selling Christian literature or just enjoy reading it depends upon their bent. Whether they become a rocket scientist or merely launch model rockets with their children depends on their giftings and motivations. Our job as homeschool parents is to provide a thorough sampling of subjects requiring minimum proficiency while allowing our children to flourish to their heart's content in the areas of their specific interest.

[Diana's maxim: Nobody knows EVERYTHING about EVERYTHING. Instead of striving for that unattainable goal, let's learn something about most things and learn lots about some things.]

Recommended Reading

To begin, read biographies and autobiographies of people you admire in history. It is liberating to see how these people were taught and how they were prepared for their life's work. (Abraham Lincoln's childhood is a good case in point.) The more you expose yourself to the many ways people were educated in history, and the more models of education you explore, the better your opportunity of finding the right method of educating your unique children.

Life Skills

Back to Basics by Reader's Digest
> A wonderful book filled with the old-fashioned ways of providing one's own needs. Learn how to build a log cabin, raise rabbits (and skin them!), make butter, survive in the wilderness, and more.

The Joy of Cooking by Irma S. Rombauer and Marion R. Becker

  Although I own dozens of cookbooks, this is the tried-and-true, never-to-be-without resource. Our children need to know where to look it up, figure it out, and fix it when it comes to cooking, and this is the best book I know!

Is There Life After Housework? by Don Aslett

  This book revolutionized the way we clean our house! I use it as the textbook for teaching my children how to clean the toilet, dust, etc. It entertains us while teaching how the pros accomplish so much in so little time.

  For sources pertaining to history, science, art, music, etc., refer to Chapter Nine.

Chapter 5

⟨∞⟩

Surviving Your First Homeschool Convention

We watched the young homeschool mother walking by, her eyes glazed, her countenance weary. As she noticed our sympathetic glance, she quickly changed direction and came straight to us.

"Do you... uh... homeschool?" she asked earnestly. When we replied affirmatively, she began to lay all of her packages down on the counter. With tears in her eyes she asked, homeschooler to homeschooler, "Where do I start? What do I do? How do I know what to buy? With all these different exhibits, I'm totally overwhelmed—can you help?"

So began a two-hour conversation, conducted partly at our booth and partly in the hall outside. Slowly but surely, this new homeschool mother began to exhibit a growing confidence that she could make her own decisions about what to buy, based on her family's unique needs. We finished talking, we prayed together, she purchased a few titles, like *You CAN Teach Your Child Successfully* and *For the Children's Sake*, and then left our booth. I saw her visit several other vendors, where she asked questions, carefully examined materials, and purchased several items.

At the next year's homeschool convention, we noticed an energetic, smiling young mother making her way determinedly into our booth. She bounced up to me, grabbed my hand, and shook it. We had visited with many thousands of homeschoolers since our last visit to this city, and frankly, I had no idea who was shaking my hand, or why!

The woman reminded me of our conversation the previous year, and then enthusiastically proclaimed, "Thank you for your advice! We LOVED school this year! It was wonderful!! My children have enjoyed learning so much, and our "school" was a tremendous success. This time, I know just what books I want and just where to find them!" With that, she again pumped my hand, bought a few books, and left.

Our Journal

"You know, Diana, if you teach a workshop, you get in free to the convention!"

I was sitting at Joan's kitchen table on a sunny winter day in January 1989. We'd been discussing the upcoming Washington State Homeschool Convention to be held during the spring in Tacoma. Although I had received inviting brochures for the past two years about this convention, I never had any extra money to spend on a convention three hours away from home. Joan had taught workshops on homeschooling the previous years and was very enthusiastic about the benefits of attending a large convention with its accompanying exhibit hall. She explained that conventions were a wonderful place to meet other homeschoolers, hear nationally known speakers, and examine curriculums up close and personal. When I reminded her of the pitiful state of my checkbook, she encouraged me to submit workshop proposals to the convention organizers, since chosen workshop providers not only got in free but also received $50 for teaching *plus* gas mileage!

I was very motivated but had no idea what I could offer to other homeschoolers. I had taught guitar lessons, gourmet cooking classes, my own children, yet somehow, none of those seemed appropriate for a homeschool convention! Joan, always the organized one, pulled out the previous year's workshop schedule to start my creative juices flowing. Going through this list, I saw that there was very little offered in the subject of music. Then I noticed that history had also received very little attention. Since those two were my favorite subject areas, I wondered whether there was something that might combine them into one workshop. Hmmm…music and history, history and music…American music and American history…hmmm…What if one were to combine American folk songs—such as *O Susanna, Yankee Doodle,* and *The Erie*

Canal—with their place in American history, with their story of a time, a place, a people? Why not?!!

The rest, as they say, is history. I called a very creative friend, Tad Suckling, the owner of a recording studio, and pitched an idea to him: What if we were to make a recording of American folk music and a book, which I could write, to sell along with it to tell the stories of these folk songs in history? (You see, I needed something for "show and tell" during my workshop.) Tad thought it was so different—off the wall, I believe was the term he used—that it might just sell. He called two other friends, Craig Russell and John Standefer, excellent studio musicians, to join us. We formed Hear & Learn Publications with the express purpose of creating educational products that were high quality, interesting, informative, and fun. Our first project was *History Alive! Through Music—America.* Tad, John, and Craig finished the tape in early May and began duplicating. I researched and wrote the book and found a typesetter, an artist, and a printer. Bill and I picked up the completed books, along with the newly duplicated tapes, the night *before* the convention.

A few hours before the convention was due to start, we arrived and madly began setting up our display of tapes, books, and miniature covered wagon. My workshop for *History Alive! Through Music* had been accepted several months before, but being a charter member of the organizationally impaired, there I was also trying to organize my notes, music, and mind for the presentation to come. We were a little scared, a little overwhelmed, a little nervous and very excited about what was going to happen in this experiment.

To my amazement, more and more people flocked to our table to hear our music (which we played continuously on the tape recorder.) As we explained that this was a product connecting American music with American history, people became very enthusiastic and began BUYING!!!! By the end of the weekend, we had sold more than one hundred tape/book sets, and we were ecstatic!

As vendors at our first homeschool convention, we felt successful. As homeschoolers at our first homeschool convention, we felt stretched. Bill and I had each tried to go around the entire exhibit hall learning of new books; looking at curriculums; talking to authors, scientists, and speakers; seeing educational games, computers, storyboard felts, and many other educational supplements. It was overwhelming to discover how much educational "stuff" was out there.

However, in the midst of the torrential outpouring of materials, we picked up some real gems. Bill discovered a vendor with Made for Trade, an educational game about a colonial village. I met Rob Evans, the Doughnut Man, and learned about children's ministry in humorous music. We visited for hours with David and Shirley Quine of Cornerstone Curriculum, Inc., since their booth was right next to ours. We closely examined several programs that we were considering using, thereby avoiding needless expenditures on unsuitable materials. I found several wonderful living books for our children that I had never heard of before. We gained insight into numerous art, grammar, music, and math programs that would benefit us in the future.

Although my workshop was the only one I had the opportunity to attend, there was a tremendous amount of shared information that came my way during the convention. Friends would stop by and tell me about something they had just learned during a workshop or about what a speaker had discussed. We learned that all the workshops were taped and that for a minimal price we could "listen in" on any presentation we wanted.

All in all, it was a marvelous, exciting, stimulating, developing experience for us. In fact, it was so wonderful that we decided to do it again the next weekend. That late spring and early summer we went to Tacoma, Spokane, Portland, and Los Angeles. The following year we added Oklahoma, Texas, and Florida to our circuit, as well as a new tape/book to our product line.

Since that summer, we've exhibited at over sixty state homeschool conventions. Because of this unique opportunity to see many different conventions around the country, get to know many of the exhibitors, and talk to several thousand homeschoolers, we've learned some of the ins and outs of surviving (and profiting from) a homeschool convention. Hoping this will be of service to you, here's our "two bits worth."

With Internet and Support Groups, Why Go?

Have you ever heard someone recount a personal past experience and finish with the statement, "Well, I guess you shoulda' been there!"? *That* is the dynamic of a homeschool convention. There is something so encouraging, so enlarging, so invigorating about attending a trade convention designed for homeschoolers that it simply cannot be duplicated by any other means.

What are the ingredients that contribute so greatly to the dynamic of a homeschool convention? It begins with an exhibit hall stocked full of vendors catering specifically to the needs of the homeschooling family, kind of like a shopping mall just for you! Then there are the main speakers, people nationally known for their expertise in areas of interest to homeschoolers. Supplementing the information and encouragement offered by the main speakers are workshops abundantly covering numerous aspects of homeschooling, a veritable banquet of knowledge and experience for us all. An added dynamic to all of this is the fellowship potential with others who have made the same lifestyle and educational choices. You may meet them at a workshop, across from you at the snack tables, or sitting on a bench studying the convention schedule. All of these individual parts combine to make a tremendously powerful and exciting whole. Homeschool conventions are a wonderful place to be.

Starting with the exhibit hall, a homeschooling family, whether new or veteran, has the opportunity to see a vast array of materials appropriate to its task. Many times, the authors of books or curriculums are available at the site to answer questions, describe specific benefits, and help you to know how to use their program. Many vendor/authors are veteran homeschoolers who have extensive experience using the materials they sell. They can share their own experiences in using these materials with their children. From their presentation you can determine with certainty whether the product will work for your family.

A very helpful aspect of the exhibit hall is the opportunity it provides to examine several different approaches to teaching certain subjects. For instance, you will find art programs that focus on studying the masterpieces, others that teach drawing from perspective, and still others that use cartooning as the primary vehicle to introduce art to children. In math you will see everything from a standard textbook with teacher's manual to a family-style, game-oriented approach to mathematics. In history, you have the option of starting your young children off with world history or American history, with Christian textbooks or literature, with music or coloring, and more. All this variety, instead of being confused or cluttered, will seem invaluable after you've read about learning style distinctions in the next chapter.

Even if you have already read every review, asked every homeschooler in your support group, and consulted your checkbook, so that you feel supremely convinced of the purchases you intend to make, I still recommend that you carefully examine the materials available in the exhibit hall. You might find something that's absolutely perfect that none of your friends have discovered. There might be a brand-new publisher with the hottest new curriculum around, but the reviews haven't come out yet! (That is exactly what happened with *5 in a Row* in 1994). You might find a fabulous special convention price on something you didn't think you could afford but now can. Picture this as the best treasure hunt you've ever been on!

If you seek diligently, you will find amazing gems in an exhibit hall. Just because one reviewer doesn't rave about a product does not mean that it might not be a jewel for you. Conversely, if a reviewer says that something is absolutely, categorically the best program around, check it out for yourself to make sure it suits you. We learned this particular lesson the hard—and expensive—way. Again, there's nothing like being there to examine products, talk to vendors, question authors, and discover new treasures.

Instruction and information about homeschooling are offered at a convention through the invited speakers and workshop presenters. Convention organizers do their very best to bring in exceptional speakers, people who have an important message to share with the homeschooling convention. We have heard such diverse topics as "Is There Life After Housework?" and "God's Mandate for Families." There have been speeches on apprenticeship, penmanship, courtship, discipleship, and "not jumping ship." There are challenge, vision, direction, and encouragement to be gained from listening to the speakers. It is thrilling to listen, for instance, to Michael Farris or Chris Klicka from Home School Legal Defense Association talk about the current political situations and what lies ahead for homeschoolers. You might hear from scientists, from public school teachers, from homeschooling authors, even from former U.S. Vice Presidents (Dan Quayle spoke to homeschoolers in Denver, Colorado in 1995.).

One of the most outstanding aspects of a homeschool convention is the wonderful variety of relevant workshops. You will find many, many helpful topics being addressed in these workshops such as "Getting Started," "Teaching Music," "Homeschooling Children with Learning Disabilities," "Multilevel Teaching." The moms, dads, local professionals, and vendors who teach these workshops are full of ideas, encouragements, and experiences. Through their instruction, you can gain tremendous vision, learn valuable tips, and receive the supportive words that you need to carry on your task.

With regard to these wonderful speakers, may I issue a challenge to you? Be a "Berean" homeschooler. Search God's Word about what a speaker has said to see whether it's true. Don't accept unquestioningly the word of experts, but seek out verification of the view they are promoting. Ask other professionals, for instance, the author/vendors in the exhibit hall, and other homeschoolers for their input. Read articles and how-to books by various experts. Unfortunately, even among nationally known homeschooling speakers, there may be wolves in sheep's clothing. Though a person may be an influential speaker with tremendous charisma, always remember that "it ain't necessarily so." So, again, be a Berean: ask the Lord for wisdom, insight, and discernment.

One of the most uplifting and valuable parts of attending a homeschool convention is the aspect of physically being with several hundred or several thousand other homeschooling families. Since, as homeschoolers, we spend most of our time at home, teaching our children in an individualized atmosphere, we may come to feel isolated and alone. But there is such strength, such encouragement, such vision when we see with our own eyes the multitudes of others who have made the same choice. There will be someone in that crowd who needs to see you, to ask your opinions, to hear your accounts, your discoveries.

I have heard from professionals in other areas that going to their trade convention every year is like a shot in the arm; a time of fellowship; an opportunity for fresh vision and new ideas; a time of sharing experiences, failures, and victories. It's a time of solidarity, a time of looking around at all the other assembled people and saying, "I belong here; I am one of them."

If this is true of doctors, retailers, builders, and realtors, how much more is it true of homeschoolers? Do you need fresh vision? Do you need encouragement? Do you feel it is important to stand together in solidarity as homeschoolers? Could you yourself be an encouragement, a blessing, a help to another homeschooler? Volunteer to help the convention workers. Could you use some new products, new approaches and new ideas? Could you use some verification or support for your efforts? Then come to a homeschool convention and experience the joy of being there.

Survival Tips

1) Wear good, comfortable walking shoes. I know that might sound obvious, but believe me, if your feet are killing you as you hustle around

an exhibit hall, your time won't be profitable. You need to come prepared to walk for *miles* (well, it seems like it) if your convention is anything like the ones we've been to. Most conventions set up the main speakers and workshops a fair distance from the exhibit hall, and you are going to want to have the option of making that trip more than once. We suggest making at least two trips through the exhibit hall—once for browsing, the second time for purchasing. Many times people want to run to the exhibit hall to purchase a product that has been mentioned during a workshop. So, come physically prepared for a walking marathon.

2) Bring a canvas shopping bag, backpack, or basket for purchases. Since many vendors do not provide shopping bags, people struggle carrying around several books, construction paper, art supplies, maps, and rubber stamps through a crowded exhibit hall. The results can be disastrous! Or even worse, when those people stop at the next booth, they set down some of their purchases and end up leaving them behind. As a homeschool version of the Boy Scouts, "Be prepared."

3) If at all possible, leave your younger children at home. Now, hear me out. We used to balk and resist and cry, "Heresy!" However, at this stage of the game, we see this as particularly sensible. Many conventions require this, and it is usually very good advice. The reason for it is that conventions are often very crowded, very busy, and very businesslike. Young children can distract you (at least mine can distract me!) at a time when you need all of your faculties intact. Think of it as your professional training time, your opportunity to become equipped for the following year, your chance to plan the very best possible school your children could ever have. This kind of "think-tank" time is best done without other responsibilities. Make it a time of refreshment, renewal, and reenergizing for the next year.

4) Have a plan. It is not possible to do it all, yet people often kill themselves trying. You cannot possibly hear every speaker, attend every workshop, and see every vendor in the exhibit hall. Rather than wear yourself out trying to take it all in, which ends in utter frustration, try to plan realistically what you most want to accomplish. When you receive the convention handouts, take the opportunity to study the schedule and various offerings. How much time is allotted for main speakers? How many workshop times are there? Is there any specially designated time

for the exhibit hall? Decide on the schedule you will follow to achieve *your* priorities.

We have found that not all conventions are created equal. Sometimes the emphasis is on main speakers, and there is little time for anything else. Other times, there are more workshops than you can shake a stick at, and you could spend all of your time hurrying from one workshop to another. Occasionally, we have found conventions with a good ratio of speaker to workshop to shopping time.

What freedom and satisfaction come from realizing that you are in charge of you—that you can design your own schedule. It is usually possible to purchase, at minimal price, tapes of all the workshops and, sometimes, even the main speakers. Would your time be better spent attending one or two workshops that most interest you, listening to one or two of the main sessions, and using the rest of the allotted time to canvas the exhibit hall? Or perhaps it would work best for you to spend one entire day (of a two-day convention) in the exhibit hall and the second day attending main sessions and workshops. Avail yourself of what is offered, but be sure to leave enough time for the things you need to accomplish.

Some special friends of ours, David and Gerri Christian, attend the Michigan homeschool convention together. Their plan is to divide up the workshops between them so that they can accomplish twice as much. This frees up much more time for the exhibit hall, main speakers, and ministry to other homeschoolers. Their motto is "Divide and conquer!" That's good advice!

5) Do your homework before you come. Read Cathy Duffy's and Mary Pride's books, recent reviews in homeschooling magazines, and vendor catalogs to find which programs and titles interest you. Write down these titles and any pertinent questions you wish to ask about them in a spiral-bound notebook. Also note your children's interests, their current level of study, and your general plan of attack for the upcoming year (e.g. more music, something in economics, projects and books for the Renaissance time period, carpentry). As you walk through the exhibit hall, make a notation of which vendors carry the products you are interested in. Make notes on any new discoveries you find, answers you've received, and the strengths and weaknesses of a program you have examined. Then, with notebook in hand, have lunch with your spouse or fellow homeschooler and talk over what you've learned. That

way, you can walk back into the exhibit hall with a sense of purpose and direction; most importantly, you can make wise purchases for your family.

I've heard veteran homeschoolers tell newcomers, "Don't bring your checkbook with you to a convention." I disagree! Conventions are a great place to *save* money and frustration as you get a chance to look through the different programs described in catalogs and homeschooling books. The trick is to hold onto your checkbook until you've made a thorough search for your priorities. Once you find the gems, the treasures, you can buy them with great assurance and delight. From our observation, here's an overlooked yet crucial idea: purchasing from onsite vendors who have served you is a tremendous blessing to them.

Servants to You

Have you ever wondered about where all these wonderful home-schooling products come from? Who are these people standing behind the table in their exhibit booths? Who are these people producing these wonderful catalogs in the convention bags? Why are they here at a home-school convention? Having spent virtually all of my time as an exhibitor at sixty-some conventions, I hold these questions near and dear to my heart.

In an ever-increasing way, products are being produced for the homeschool market by *homeschool parents*. As a homeschool mom works with her children, she discovers a new way of teaching history, which she shares with other homeschoolers on audiocassette. As another homeschool mom sends the last of her children off to college, new homeschoolers beg her to show them "how to," and a new "beginner's curriculum" is born. A homeschooling dad looks at the grammar pro-grams available on the market and decides to use his expertise in lin-guistics to create a more usable model of grammar. These are but a few of the true stories behind some of the best educational materials avail-able for homeschoolers.

These homeschooling families spend a tremendous amount of time, trouble, and effort to produce something to benefit you. Unlike some of the materials available on the market, these writers have no major text-book publisher behind them paying the way. They have often invested their life savings to publish these materials and now wait upon God for the return. You will make an incredible difference in their lives as you patronize their products at conventions and through the mail. The laborer is worthy of his hire; to whatever extent these workers help you, bless them.

Most exhibiting companies are homeschoolers themselves, or employ homeschooling families, just like you and me. Many travel from convention to convention, spending tremendous amounts of money for exhibit booths, travel expenses, van breakdowns, food, and inventory. Others spend an enormous sum to serve the homeschooling community by providing fabulous catalogs which bring what you need throughout the year right to your door. We have had the blessing of getting to know many of these precious families and know firsthand that they are not getting rich quick. In fact, they are not getting rich at all. If an exhibitor at a convention makes any profit at all, it is a blessing from God and received with great thankfulness! Don't let all those books, games, tapes, etc., fool you. Most of the exhibitors are not there to get rich. These families are here as servants, to serve you, and are working diligently to avoid going broke. The laborer is worthy of his hire.

One final point along this line is this: if exhibitors spend time with you, answering your questions about this curriculum and that book, if they help you evaluate your children's current levels, then BUY THE BOOK FROM THEM! Remember, the laborer is worthy of his hire. If someone has served you, worked for you, labored for you, then bless that person—even if it means spending 50¢ more, even if it means waiting for them to send it in the mail. The principle of giving and receiving is at work here, a principle of the Kingdom. We are to be good stewards, yes, but we are also called to bless those who labor among us. The laborer is worthy of his hire.

Your first homeschool convention! You have your running shoes on, your backpack empty, your notebook in hand. Ask the Lord for wisdom, discernment, patience, and joy for your adventure. Then, go for it! And God bless you!!

Recommended Reading

First recommendation: if at all possible, read Cathy Duffy's and Mary Pride's books. They will help you to know what's out there to have a good basis to begin.

Second recommendation: read as many catalogs from homeschool suppliers as you can find. These materials will prepare you with ideas of what's available from whom and for how much and may introduce you to new products that have just been released.

Third recommendation: when you read someone's book on home-schooling, note any suggested reading. Prepare yourself a good foundation by reading books, recommended by authors you trust, about various topics, such as education, organization, family, how to teach_____, scheduling, etc.

Part Two

⌒⌒⌒

The Journey

Chapter 6

❦

Different Strokes
for Different Folks
Learning Styles

*T*he anxious young couple sat in the very last row of the auditorium where Bill was vividly presenting a workshop called "Learning Styles." As the presentation rollicked along in Bill's humorous, inimitable style, the couple sat up straighter, then leaned forward eagerly in their seats. The look on their faces became one of joy and relief, and we wondered what was taking place in this young couple's heart and mind.

At the appropriate place in his workshop, Bill began to talk about Isaac, our son. He shared about the amazing difference we began to see in Isaac when we utilized what we were studying about learning styles and modalities. Our classic example was the issue of cleaning his bedroom.

The story goes like this. I used to look Isaac straight in the eye and tell him very plainly, "Make your bed, pick up your clothes, straighten your bookshelves, put away your toys, and take your muddy shoes downstairs." For me, that list was very understandable, very logical, and easily remembered. But for my seven-year-old son it was impossible, something akin to memorizing the entire Old Testament in one setting. Since it was so easy for me, I assumed it was easy for Isaac. Imagine my astonishment and displeasure as I walked into his room thirty minutes later and discovered that out of my entire to-do list, only his bed was made. It just seemed like such willful disobedience on his part, and frankly, this upset me every time it happened, though I did everything I could think of to teach him to mind.

Then one day, Bill brought home some materials on how children take in, process, and learn information. When we read about visual learners and how they take in information through sight rather than through hearing, something clicked inside of me. Isaac had shown himself to be very visual, whereas I am very auditory. Could this difference possibly be at the root of our problem?

The next time room cleaning was on the agenda, we made a written list for Isaac. The list had all the same specifics that I used to *say* to him, but they were all on paper with a place for checking them off as accomplished. To our utter amazement, Isaac cleaned his entire room by himself for the very first time and took great delight in checking off each of the "to do's."

When Bill finished the story, he asked for questions or comments. The hands of the young couple in the back row shot up excitedly. Then jumping to her feet, the mother joyfully shouted, "You mean my daughter isn't bad?!!"

With dawning hope she explained, "You see, we have been really confused about our little girl. She is sweet and very loving in all other respects, but she sometimes is disobedient to our verbal commands. We have tried punishing our daughter, scolding her, restricting her, talking to her, and *nothing* has helped, *nothing* has changed. But what you described today about your son sounds exactly like what we've been dealing with. And to think that this may have all been a difference in how she learns!"

With that, she broke down and cried. Her husband, with his new-found understanding, said, "Boy, are there going to be some big changes around our house!"

Our Journal

During the past two years, we've become more and more aware of the different ways our children approach a looming deadline. This has given us insight into their unique blend of learning styles and has given rise to much silent hilarity on our part.

Melody, our vivacious, red-headed ten-year-old, has proven to be the most organized person in our household. When she is assigned a project, she jumps into it immediately and with gusto. Melody does research in our personal library, the city library, and, through the aid of the post office, the state library. She methodically plots her strategy: what kind of presentation best fits this subject—drama, art, speech, written report, table display, charts? She then painstakingly carries out her strategy in all of the detail required by her artistic nature. Most amazing (to me), her project/report is *always* finished ahead of time.

Michael, our tenacious "mountain man," does not eagerly receive an assignment that requires lots of research and writing. Though he *loves* to research and compare prices on sleeping bags, hiking shoes, camping stoves, and fishing poles, he feels that having to research a presentation on economics is much less interesting and more of a cramp in his style. Though he will spend days and nights reading about World War II through the adventurous eyes of submarine captains and fighter pilots, he finds reading a textbook on the war to be the antidote for insomnia! Though he goes into high gear when I ask him to create a present from leather or make cinnamon rolls or start a fire in the woodstove, he hesitates to sit down and write out a report on weather—such an assignment stretches him beyond his comfort zone. So, when he is given an assignment, it has been imperative that we put our collective homeschooling heads together. We look for a way that Michael can present what he has learned that utilizes his strengths and interests (which might mean carving the title of his report in leather). And we recognize that we need to encourage him in this assigned work every single day.

Then there's Isaac, our "absent-minded professor." When given an assignment, he shows great enthusiasm and immediately figures out his approach to this presentation. He orders a few books from the library and sets them carefully on his shelf. Then he goes on his merry way without giving it another thought! One or two days before his required presentation, he'll smack the side of his head and say, "Oh my gosh, I forgot!" With great energy, dexterity, and creativity, he crams several weeks' worth of work into twenty-four hours and finishes his project. His presentations are usually very, very articulate and interesting, but the ink on the paper is still dripping.

I often feel as if I'm living on the racetrack of the tortoise and the hare, with the interesting addition of a racing ant. When given a three-week deadline, Melody industriously moves right through her assignment and finishes within the first week; Michael plods along, day by day, with the tenacity of a bulldog, ending his work on the day it is due; and Isaac cheerily takes "just a minute to lie down for a little rest" and then jumps up wildly for a mad dash to the finish line.

I cannot criticize Isaac very much, because that is MY style, too. When I attended college, I found it much easier to accomplish my work if I waited until a few days before the deadline. It's patently obvious to my family that I create best under pressure. (Actually, I don't create at all if I'm not under pressure!) This used to make me angry with myself until, in my study of history, I discovered many other inventive people who had the same need for pressure in order to create.

Bill takes the more methodical route to accomplishing a project. He works steadily from day one until the deadline, finishing off at just the right time. He "plans his work and works his plan." This style works wonderfully for him, and bores me to tears!

You could compare our difference in style with, for the one, sailing on a lake when it's peaceful and calm, making steady but slow progress, or, for the other, waiting until the winds reach hurricane proportions— it's a wild and scary ride, but the trip is made in record time.

What a wonderful gift God has given us in our diversity and differences! We learn so much as we make allowance for the other person's ways, and as some of their style rubs off on us, we become more well rounded. Bill's steady, methodical pursuit has rubbed off on me enough that I have gained the ability to sit down and write this book day after day after day (though it *does* help to know I have a deadline looming). Only after sixteen years of marriage has this been possible for me, the "queen of the immediate." On the other hand, my wild and crazy ways have helped Bill to be willing to attempt a project on the spur of the moment. That's why we now have a beautiful, wooden homeschool bookshelf spanning our kitchen wall. The day I decided I needed it, Bill went out and threw some boards together. I raced out a few hours later to sand and varnish the wood, bring the bookshelf into the house for a few hours to dry, and then load the books onto it. The bookshelf turned out wonderfully, though Bill has mentioned a few times that he wished he had had a couple of more days to assemble it properly. At the time, I didn't want "proper," I wanted "now," and Bill was able to adjust his style accordingly.

So, you see, we are learning that each one in our family has a valuable style, one that we can all learn from. Melody's industrious, organized ways have become invaluable to me, since she plans out most of our holiday celebrations, birthdays, and other special times. She always reminds me that it's time to plan for this or that, whereas I would usually remember an event on the day it occurs. Previously, and on more than one occasion, we had wrapped presents with the Sunday comics, in the car, on the way to a birthday party, but with Melody's giftedness in this area, that is a thing of the past. Hallelujah!

Michael's diligent attention, his tenacity with detail, and his ability to make things happen with his hands have also become utterly necessary for the smooth functioning of our home. He fixes things for me, builds the fire in the woodstove (though all of us know how, he just has a knack for making it go), cooks dinner at a moment's notice, and stretches me past my comfort zone when it comes to camping, backpacking, hunting, and fishing. As he studies the Russian language, he teaches it to me in great detail (whether I want to know it or not!). His style, though very different from mine, is a *gift* to our family and is causing us to grow.

Isaac's free-wheeling ideas and creativity have opened up whole new horizons for us. His artistry has kept us in laughter as he cartoons, in peaceful rest as he plays worship choruses, and in suspense as he writes mysteries. His breakneck speed in finishing a project just before the deadline has given me a few gray hairs, but it is part and parcel of the gifting God has given him. I am hoping that he will learn some moderation and pacing from his father's style, but, as I know from personal experience, that takes time.

Let us grow together in grace, learning to appreciate our God-given diversity and to respect our differences in styles. How can you grow in this appreciation and respect if you haven't yet learned about these different learning styles? Good question! On to the "good stuff."

Simply Stated

In the past several years, many different designations and explanations have been offered for learning/personality styles. These styles are given Greek names, animal names, esoteric names, and number names. Some of the describers of these different styles have been psychologists working from a humanist perspective, while others have been Christian counselors who see God's design in our differences. Books are available that describe, among other things, learning styles, personality styles, the "seven intelligences," learning modalities, and right brain/left brain differences.

With this plethora of information, how do we sift out what's useful for us? Is it possible to avoid overlabeling our children and spouse while still growing in understanding and appreciation of their differences? And can somebody please make this SIMPLE???!!!!

While Bill was preparing to teach workshops on learning styles to homeschoolers, I confessed to still not having a grasp of the concept of different styles—it felt like trying to grab ahold of a particularly well-greased pig! As soon as I thought I was beginning to understand, poof, it shot out of my mind and left me confused. Bill decided that his presentation needed to be so simple that ANYONE would be able to understand and apply the elements of the different types of learners.

What this simplifying required was to utilize all our knowledge of the various means that people use to process information. Some people process most comfortably when they see something (visual), others when they hear something (auditory), and still others when they can touch, open, make, or pick up something (kinesthetic). We decided to illustrate the learning styles by using vivid, colorful fabric for the visual, classical music for the auditory, and a display of books and various items that could be picked up for the kinesthetic.

It was incredible how much these little helps made a difference in being able to grasp the somewhat complex material being covered. For the first time, I understood and could rattle off the major differences between learning styles, and I was able to readily use this information in my own home. As we traveled around the country, many families told us that they finally "got it!" when it came to understanding learning styles.

Under the obvious limitations of trying to communicate the gist of Bill's dramatic presentation in written form, I invite you to come along for an introduction, unlike any you've ever had, to the wild and wonderful world of learning styles.

The terms used in this particular grouping of learning styles—thinker, feeler, sensor, intuitor—were developed by a researcher named Meyers-Briggs over a twenty-year time frame. Alta Vista school uses this classification in its homeschool unit study materials. It recently published a wonderful resource, based on the Meyers-Briggs terms, called *Learning Style and Tools*. If you are familiar with a different group of names or some different groupings of characteristics, perhaps you can gain some new insights into the wonderful differences God has given us when you translate these names into your own understanding (otter, beaver, golden retriever, lion; phlegmatic, choleric, melancholic, sanguine; actual spontaneous, actual routine, conceptual specific, conceptual global; D I S C; or others).

The Facts, Ma'am, Just the Facts

Picture black-and-white striped material arranged precisely, exactly, perfectly on a table, as if conforming to a well-executed master plan. (Do you know how hard it is to get stripes to stay perfectly?) Although you cannot see it, you undoubtedly know that just beyond your range of vision is a sign saying, "Do not disturb the stripes." There is something very formal, perhaps austere, about this material and the precise way it is arranged, and you look on it with tremendous respect and reserve.

Listen! Can you hear the music of Papa Haydn's *Surprise Symphony* playing impressively in the background? That is the wonderfully planned symphony designed to give a wake-up call right in the middle of the performance. Franz Joseph Haydn was a master composer during the era historians refer to as the classical period. The music of this period is precise, conforming to precise rules, logical in its flow, and understandable in form. The classical period is also a time of tremendous beauty in music, including composers such as Mozart and Beethoven. Precise, exact, well-executed, orderly music fills the air while you continue to gaze at the flawless black and white striped fabric resting precisely and perfectly on the table.

Now, do you see all those gadgets that are being placed on the material? Stopwatch, ruler, a dictionary, Robert's Rules of Order, a daily organizer, a set of encyclopedias, pocket protector, computer manuals, all set exactly and precisely in a row with a 45-degree tilt. These are the very necessities of life to the learning style designated the "thinker."

The thinker is a person who sees everything as black or white; no gray areas are considered. Thinkers are precise, exact, organized, meticulous, and scheduled. These learners respect tremendously the authority of a textbook and of a teacher. Since they are most comfortable with a textbook approach they want all the material that is to be learned to be laid out precisely, logically, and carefully. In fact, these learners will want to use very authoritative, very scholarly books for researching the *facts*. ("Thank you, but I want to know the facts rather than your opinion.") A thinker needs his/her teacher to have a clear and logical plan for each subject and wants to know precisely when school will start, when it will end, and how much is expected to be accomplish. This person generally enjoys making lists and putting sets of materials into order. Because this learning style expects perfection of itself, when you assign a project you must give an adequate amount of time for completion. If you plan to give a test on what the person has been studying, give the person a thorough chance to prepare (pop quizzes are *not* comfortable!).

If you are a thinker, you are probably nodding your head in agreement with all of these statements, seeing the absolute "rightness" of being precise and exact and of living your life according to a well-scheduled routine. You relate completely to Phileas Fogg, Jules Verne's precisionally perfect character in *Around the World in Eighty Days*. If you are not a thinker, you may think these people are unemotional, cold, and stuffy. A thinker's desire for logic, order, precision, and factual information may make you want to run for a breath of fresh air and a quick bit of spontaneity.

Remember, God has created us—and it's His wisdom that has made us so different from one another. If you are having difficulty appreciating this learning style, which might belong to your spouse, your child, your in-laws, ask God to make it clear to you *how* this is a gift to your family!

People Who Need People

Now picture a beautiful swath of luscious red velvet draped becomingly over a small table for two in a candlelit room. This luscious fabric draws you into the picture, creating a longing to remain in that warm, inviting spot. Just imagine the wonderful conversations between dear friends that such a sumptuous setting would inspire.

As you contemplate the scene, the heartfelt strains of Tchaikovsky's *Romeo and Juliet* fade into the background. A swelling, stirring emotion rises in your heart as you listen to this beautiful music from the Romantic era. Written for the ballet based upon Shakespeare's tragedy of two despairing lovers, this piece is some of the most beautiful emotional music the world has ever known, and it perfectly fits this rich, luxuriant scene.

Observe, now, the waiters coming to the table, bearing some unusual items for this setting. Gleaming silver platters contain biographies, historical fiction, and other books concerning people. Enhancing the scene is a crystal vase overshadowed by the lovely, fragrant red rose it contains. You also see a stethoscope, an anthology of poetry, a singalong tape of math drills, giftwrap, masterpieces of portrait art, and a whole bowl full of warm fuzzies. (I can't describe warm fuzzies, I just know they make you feel good!) These elements all belong to the learning style of the feeler—the one concerned with others, the people person.

The feeler is the one who really *can't* learn if he/she is agitated in a significant relationship, such as with his/her teacher. This learner asks, "How does this subject affect people—does it make any difference at all in my life or in the lives of others?" Decisions are made based on the people perspective—"Is this good for us, for them?"—rather than on cold, hard facts. Up-close and personal stories are the feeler's favorite introduction to any subject. Feelers can be expected to accomplish any sort of project or activity, but only after its importance has been established and they have had a chance to explain how they feel about it.

To interest a feeler in science, have him/her read biographies of such scientists as Isaac Newton or Louis Pasteur. Emphasize the impact and results of an invention rather than its mechanical complexities. Feelers would especially enjoy the heartwarming stories of Clara Barton and Florence Nightingale as a way to study the history of the 1800s, because these two pioneering nurses helped other people. Rather than using a bare-bones textbook approach to the American Revolution, a feeler would prefer to read *Johnny Tremain*, biographies of George Washington, and Longfellow's "Paul Revere's Ride," or help build a model of Concord Town. If they are bogging down in math because they just can't get interested, reading *Mathematicians Are People, Too* or *Carry On, Mr. Bowditch*, or singing with the Skip-Count-Kids will get feelers jumpstarted.

Nothing is more wonderful to a feeler than cuddling up on a couch to read together, to study together, to talk together, to be together—notice that the key word here is *together*. When a feeler is in the midst of an unresolved conflict with others (no matter how minor), no learning can take place, no thought processes are possible. You might as well put away the books until the situation can be brought to a peaceful conclusion.

If you are a feeler, you probably want to sit down for that cup of tea with a friend right now. You find it easy to identify with the emotions and actions of the title character in *Pollyanna*. If you are a thinker, you are thinking, "Not *me*, thank the Lord!" Yet do you see how these two learning styles have much to offer us all? Without the people perspective of the feeler, this world would be a very cold, unfeeling place in which to live, and without the thinker, without his or her knowledge of the under-girding structure of facts, we might live in a "jellyfish" world! Though these two learning styles seem direct opposites, speaking two mutually incomprehensible languages, God in His wisdom has put them both on the earth, and often in the same family. So let's continue to ask Him how to grow in understanding and appreciating one another, since this is all His idea anyway.

See the Hill, Take the Hill

Wham! Bang! Whop! Ziz! A blur of vivid colors goes whizzing by the next table. These colors appear to be attached to a person, but they are moving so quickly you're not sure just what you are seeing. The next moment, lickety-split, the table is turned upside down. This especially capable person adjusts the table legs so they won't wobble, then turns the table right side up, dusts it off, and zooms on to the next project.

Beyond the sounds of fast-paced activity, you hear the music from the ballet *Rodeo* coming through the speakers. This energetic, lively music makes you want to do-si-do all around the room. *Rodeo* is an all-American, full-of-life, cowboy-inspired, captivating piece of music by America's own composer, Aaron Copland. It captures the unique essence of the American West, with its demand for hard work and common sense. The musical depiction of this boundless energy expresses perfectly all the action taking place at that table.

Suddenly, a "white tornado" zips by and deftly arranges several items on the table for this learning style. Rulers, scissors, T squares, rope, a hot glue gun, nails, a hammer, How-to books, "Design a" books, wallpaper samples, and paintbrushes all wait to be used. All of these hands-on, fixer-upper, project-oriented tools belong to the learning style of the sensor.

The sensor is a take-charge kind of person, a "let's get this done RIGHT and get it done NOW" kind of learner. Practical and efficient, the sensor learning style wants to see the here-and-now use and application. Working with their hands is better than sitting and doing bookwork. In fact, for younger sensor children, sitting still is just about impossible. Sensors will do very well in their studies if you allow them to move, to pick things up, to jump, to march, to fiddle with something while they listen (which tends to make some teachers think they couldn't *possibly* be learning anything). Committing thoughts to paper is very difficult for sensors. Recognizing that fact will help you to serve them. When possible, give them a demonstration project rather than a written report to express what they've learned. Make written reports more interesting by allowing them to add wood carvings, cartoons, clippings, drawings, playdough replicas of the Mayflower, whatever helps them learn.

Study the Battle of Waterloo using not textbooks or fiction but stuffed animals, miniature soldiers (like G.I. Joes), and other hands-on, moveable toys. Have the children set up the battle, with all of the various armies, and then quickly examine what took place. Sensors will be in their element if they can demolish the army with a sweep of the teddy bear's foot or trounce the army with stampeding plastic horses.

The study of chemistry will become absolutely captivating if you let your children set up a chemistry lab and mix things together. (Caution: Read the labels on the chemicals to see which ones blow up!!!) Dry-ice experiments will keep a sensor happy and learning for hours. Just give the students an idea of what should happen, and let them go!

Reading can be one of the most difficult things for a sensor to do, since it requires sitting for such a long time. However, encourage their reading by giving them exciting adventure stories. Read to them lots— far beyond your own comfort level. You may have to help to develop their desire to read by reading the first part of the story to them. Then stop right at the cliff-hanger spot and set the book within their easy reach. Watch what happens next!

Gardening, sewing, woodworking, cooking, crafting, wallpapering, painting, auto mechanics, building are all areas of potential interest, excitement, and learning for the sensor. Incorporating these activities into history, grammar, or spelling allows greater comprehension in these otherwise bookish studies. Sitting, keeping still, listening for hours, and writing reports are all very, *very* difficult for the sensor and need to be modified or avoided whenever possible.

This learning style is quite different from the thinker and the feeler. If you are a sensor, you may have had to read this book in quick moments between doing your projects, while the feeler luxuriously cuddled up on the couch to read it, and the thinker sat at a desk with a pen and pad to jot down notes. And each of you highlighted a different point in each section. The thinker has a great strength in the well-thought-out planning of projects, while the sensor excels in accomplishing the projects. The feeler would be in his or her element creating harmony among people working together on a project that was supervised by a sensor and planned by a thinker.

God has created us with these intrinsic differences so that we would all *need* each other and would benefit greatly by working together. If you have a sensor in your family, give thanks to the Lord! If you are trying to homeschool a sensor, ask God for creative wisdom to utilize your child's strengths as you teach the child. Sensors are a gift from God to us all.

Let's Try Something New!

Bolts of lightning flash across the night-blue material where it was thrown across the table in a hurry. The atmosphere is charged with electricity, signifying something dramatic is about to happen. Although the fabric appears to have been placed randomly, there is something very specific, not negligent, about its arrangement. You might even think that a creative, artistic designer had simply produced a new way of setting a table—voilà!

Abruptly, the sound of music cascades over you. It is the dramatic and expressive *Symphony of the Planets* by Holst. Right now, Jupiter is the planet being depicted. Do you hear the flashes of light, the bursts of discovery in the music? It is a varied piece with some soft, subtle interludes followed by the sudden bombastic, resilient sound of brass crashing into the quiet.

Scattered across the table are spare parts, tools, a CD player with mood music, several notebooks labeled "Ideas to Pursue" and "Projects to Do," resources about whatever is of interest at that moment, "The Daydreamer's Guide to Creativity." To top it all off, draped over one corner is the most decrepit, eccentric, gaudy old flannel shirt from Grandpa's closet. These are a few of the items belonging to the intuitor learning style.

Intuitors are the what-if people. They see the possibilities, the never-before-tried methods, the "tired of the old ways, let's try something new." If you are teaching an intuitor, it is quite probable that you have already had some run-ins with this child's style of learning. For instance, when you present a carefully prepared lesson plan, the intuitor will challenge you with, "Why do you want to do it that way? How about trying it like this?" Intuitors make leaps of reason, coming to interesting, though sometimes impractical, conclusions. They sit to think and consider for a long time. You would probably call them lazy unless you were present when they leap to action. The bells ring, the cymbals clash, and they are off to put their ideas to work—or find someone who can! Intuitors are the idea generators. They manufacture idea after idea after idea. Not all their ideas are practical, usable, or reasonable, but every once in a while, they come up with world changers.

My favorite example from Bill's workshop concerns a young boy daydreaming, staring out the window. All of a sudden, a bird flies into the glass, stunning itself. This young intuitor exclaims, "Mom, a bird just flew into the window!" Then, "Mom, MOM! Our house is in the flight path of the birds!!!!" Obviously, anyone can figure out that faulty reasoning. However, a wise mother will gently walk her intuitor child down the path of reason and help him to assess the fact that very few birds hit the windows and perhaps it was the lighting that confused the bird. Then she will wait for the moment when that leap of reason results in a major breakthrough.

A good case in point is that of Nikola Tesla. In the late 1800s many people were trying to figure out a way to make electricity usable, not just at the generator but miles away from it. As Tesla was away from his lab taking a walk one day, he suddenly conceived in his mind, in a flash, in a leap of reason, the alternating current induction motor! Every expert knew it could *not* be done, but it *was* done after an intuitor had given it some thought. Tesla had made a leap of reason, skipping right over all the difficulties everyone else was facing, and produced a working model on *the very first try*. His motor revolutionized the way electricity is used.

Often accused of laziness, intuitors are generally hard at work while they sit and stare out the window. If a thinker, feeler, or sensor sits and stares, he or she is taking a break, but when intuitors sit, they're working just as hard as they can to analyze and understand what was taught. (An important point to remember, Mom!)

Just as we've seen how thinkers plan out a project, feelers help to decide which project is important, and sensors make the project happen, intuitors also have an important place in the scheme of things. They are the ones, as you may have guessed, who first come up with the idea and then figure out how to get around the obstacles. Isn't it amazing to see how we all fit jointly together, each with his/her particular strengths to contribute?

These are important concepts to dwell upon because if we forget that we have been created differently, we may criticize and condemn the ones who are not like us. In our families, it is absolutely critical to grow in appreciation for our different styles, our different ways of doing things. In fact, I am convinced that God wisely places different learning styles together in each family for our *good* and for the growth of our family.

Wide Receivers

Working together with the four different learning styles are three perceptual modalities: visual, auditory, and kinesthetic. To understand modalities, think about modes of transportation. To get across town, do you prefer to be conveyed by taxi, train, or bus? One of these will be the best mode of transportation for you. It will carry things for you according to your needs and preferences. As this concerns learning, you have a preferred mode to carry information to your mind. Do you prefer the vision mode, the hearing mode, or the handling mode? Some people acquire new material best by reading it, others by hearing it spoken aloud, and still others by touching, tasting, smelling, or feeling it. The learning styles—thinker, feeler, sensor, intuitor—describe how one behaves while learning. The perceptual modalities—visual, auditory, kinesthetic—describe how information is conveyed to the mind. It might seem overly technical, but read on. The examples will clarify it for you.

Bill became quite aware of his own perceptual modality when he began working for the brick mason. To learn the various concepts of bricklaying, the costs, the difficulties, etc., he needed to learn from Larry about what the crew was working on. Larry, a sensor who learns well through the auditory modality, began to talk. Larry was glad to speak right up and to tell Bill everything he ever wanted to know about bricklaying—and more. Bill was overwhelmed, and the whole lecture ended up making no sense to him at all. Bill asked if there was a book on bricklaying and brick design that he could study. With a puzzled look on his face, Larry handed him a mason's guide and suggested that he would never figure it out from a book.

The next day, after some intense study of the book, Bill came back with a full understanding of what the different brick designs required. Larry was astonished, Bill was pleased, and we all learned from that incident that Bill certainly learns through the visual modality.

Using the visual modality means that a person will be able to learn new information better by reading, looking at pictures, writing notes, observing, and so on, than through lecture or from a table full of tools and parts. This person will appreciate trips to the library, abundant book resources, charts, diagrams, and other visual aids.

I have long been aware that if I hear someone speak, I can remember what he or she said. It is wonderfully fulfilling for me to listen to teachers, speakers, preachers, and storytellers, since what is spoken makes so much sense to me. In fact, if I need to know something, I try to find someone who can explain it to me—out loud. I perceive through the auditory modality, which is quite a contrast to Bill's visual modality, and this difference has has led to some interesting difficulties. For instance, in the past when I needed Bill to run to the store for a few items, I would say, "Please get eggs, milk, butter, cheese... and oh, yes, salsa." He would repeat the list and hurry out the door, but by the time he reached the store he would have forgotten all but the first item on the list. I was always astonished that he could not remember a piddly number of items on a list, and he was astonished that I could. We have since learned to write things down for Bill's shopping trips, while I just speak the list out loud to myself.

Auditory perceivers need to hear new information to best receive it. They will excel by listening to speakers and teachers. You may find they thrive by listening to teaching tapes or perhaps listening to a video. (I realize most people watch videos, but those who function in the auditory mode will receive the information mainly by listening to them.)

The kinesthetic one of our house is Michael. He reminds me of Garfield, when Garfield remarks, "Anything I touch is mine!" Michael has always touched anything that interests him. I realize that most of us touch something to pick it up and examine it, but Michael takes that to new heights by poking an object, pushing it, stretching it, squishing it, bouncing it, breaking it, on and on.

The kinesthetic modality is the one in which the student receives new information best by touching an object, feeling it, smelling it, tasting it. If they want to study birds, for instance, kinesthetic learners will pick up the bird, hold its legs while it flaps, stroke its feathers, let it bite a finger. The visual perceiver is happy to study a book on birds, and an auditory one prefers to hear a lecture on birds at the local birdwatchers' meeting.

These three different "receivers," or modalities, can belong to any one of the four learning styles. For instance, you may be a thinker learner with the auditory modality, which means you prefer to receive your new information orally. Or, you may be a feeler learner with the visual modality, which means you need to receive new information by reading it. Sensors often combine with the kinesthetic modality, but this is not necessarily the case.

It is very important to note that although people learn best when they perceive new information in their modality, they can learn to use the other receivers as well. For instance, I have learned how to obtain new information from books (visual) even though I would much prefer to have someone tell me a good story (auditory). Bill works hard to learn Sunday after Sunday just by respectfully listening to the sermon, but he finds it greatly helps to take notes. Michael has learned a number of things by reading books, though his hands itch to get to the real thing.

This introduction to learning styles and perceptual modalities is merely a tiny slice of the pie. There are several excellent books on the subject, and I highly recommend reading further. Realize, too, that we are all unique, so we cannot be adequately classified into just these pigeonholes. However, with all of its limitations, generally recognizing the particular learning style and modality of your family members can take you a long way toward understanding and appreciating one another. And, as we'll see in the next chapter, it makes the job of teaching your students far easier.

Recommended Reading

Learning Styles and Tools by Alta Vista
> Very easy to follow for homeschooling parents, the book describes the four learning styles discussed in this chapter. It includes tests for determining learning styles and helpful suggestions for teaching each of them.

The Way They Learn by Cynthia Ulrich Tobias
> This book is probably the most enjoyable to read on learning styles. Cynthia's presentation is loaded with humorous examples. Not only does she explain the four learning styles (though she uses different terms than I used), she also describes different environments for learning, modalities, and the seven intelligences.

People Types and Tiger Stripes by Gordon Lawrence
> A summary of the concepts developed during Meyers-Briggs's extensive research. Not easy reading, since it is very analytical, with extensive detail. However, you will find it to be invaluable for an in-depth understanding of this subject. It is currently being applied to management/employee evaluations.

Learning Styles by Marlene D. LeFever

The best book I've read about how to teach to the different learning styles, it also has a wonderful description of the particular needs and expressions of each learning style. Though the author is primarily addressing Sunday school teachers, her principles and examples are very useful to homeschoolers.

Chapter 7

❧

Mom Is My Teacher!
Teaching Styles

Barb West is an amazing woman. She and her husband Bruce teach their two girls at home. Their girls are remarkably well-educated, thoughtful, industrious, and fun-loving. In addition to teaching her daughters, Barb (with Bruce's help) was the convention organizer in Rapid City, South Dakota, for several years, watchdog for political happenings relevant to homeschooling in that state, and state liaison for HomeSchool Legal Defense Association. She also represented the state of South Dakota at national homeschooling conferences, helped guide new homeschoolers in her area, organized homeschooling seminars, volunteered with Bruce as ski patrol worker during the winter (which required completing an EMT course), and helped to lead worship at her church. Whew!

Barb's style of teaching is very, VERY organized. In fact, her whole life is very, VERY organized. When we first sat down to visit over a plate of Chinese food, the subject of scheduling our homeschool came up. She related that she and her family get up at 5:30 a.m. during the week, eat breakfast by 6:00, and start school by 7:00 at the latest. When I asked her what on earth they ate at 6:00 in the morning (not being sure whether or not it was natural for our bodies to actually consume food at that

105

unearthly hour), she patiently explained that she prepared such things as homemade banana bread and homemade granola the previous day. Since my style is to wait until the last moment to decide that what I really want is coffee cake—which takes forty-five minutes and means that we don't eat breakfast until 9:30 or 10:00—her organization and planning were flabbergasting to me.

Another friend who knows her quite well told me that one Saturday morning Barb showed up on the doorstep at 7:00 a.m., perfectly dressed, make-up flawlessly applied, with every hair in place. My friend was bleary-eyed, still in her pajamas, her hair all askew, and was totally over-whelmed by such early morning perfection, as I was when Barb called me at 7:30 a.m. to talk over decisions for the upcoming convention. Fortunately, Barb couldn't see me through the telephone.

The house Bruce and Barb lived in was always clean and orderly, her children were always neat and clean; even Barb's purse was always clean and organized. One evening, as our families were on our way again to our favorite Chinese restaurant, my son Michael sneezed. I rummaged frantically through my disorganized purse, looking for the remnants of something resembling a Kleenex. Unable to find anything remotely suit-able, I turned in desperation to Barb and asked, "Do you happen to have a tissue in your purse?" As she calmly reached into her purse and pulled out a perfectly folded, perfectly clean new tissue, we all began to laugh. Of course she did! It was no surprise, though it was very entertaining. Barb was prepared for such an emergency—she was ALWAYS prepared.

Our Journal

I have had such a comfort, such a peace, such freedom since I began to understand my learning/teaching style. I was surrounded by friends who started at the beginning of the year, at the beginning of the books, with a laid-out plan covering the entire year. On the absolute other end of the spectrum, I preferred to start when it seemed right, using books however the mood struck, and though I had a general list of goals for the year, I simply didn't care to have a day-to-day plan of attack.

I felt terribly guilty about my lack of routine, my lack of structure, my lack of *desire* for routine and structure, until we started studying learning styles. All of a sudden, it all began to make sense. I am primar-ily an intuitor, an idea person, one who does well getting the ball started but not so well keeping the ball moving. I excelled in getting my kids excited about learning something and then struggled to see the project through to completion.

My style was very spontaneous, very interest-motivated. One autumn morning I woke up and noticed that the leaves were turning colors. "Hmmm...I wonder why they do that?" The next thing my children knew, we were off to the library, checking out books on trees, seasons, leaves, hibernation, and more. We spent hours outside collecting leaves, examining trees, and basking in the warmth of the afternoon sun. Then my husband stepped into the picture and helped us to organize our studies. Within a few weeks, our children presented an oral/visual report, "Why Leaves Change Color in the Fall."

Last year I picked up a few interesting books dealing with the American system of economics. Poof! An idea jumped into my mind about taking our children through an economics course based on these delightful and interesting books. This fall we have studied, discussed, considered, and read about mortgages, debts, small businesses, entrepreneurship, velocity, supply and demand, inflation, recession, and more. Though I knew next to nothing about these issues, I figured we could all learn together. And we have, at least, they have. After a few sessions of reading and discussing, I left the subject to my husband's capable care. Under Bill's prodding, Isaac, Michael, and Melody produced fabulous charts and diagrams illustrating the principles they had learned. (I did attend the final presentation, and I learned a lot from it.)

We are learning, as parents, how to best utilize our corporate strengths, our learning/teaching styles. My primary strength is to come up with ideas and to get our kids motivated and excited about learning. Bill's complementary strength is to keep the children on task and make sure they are learning step by step. Since Bill is seldom home during the day to oversee, he writes a "To Do" list each evening for the following day's work. Bill's strength in thinking through the logical progression for study is what enables our children to have a thorough grounding, and my strength in getting them excited about the possibilities is what keeps our school hopping.

Though we are all unique, both in our approach and in our style of teaching, it is very helpful to consider some of the basic categories we fit into and to consider how to utilize our strengths and minimize our weaknesses. Then we can go on to the subject of how to gracefully teach someone who learns in a different style from ours. Ready? Let's begin!

To Each His Own...Style!

This chapter presents some general observations about the collisions caused by differences in learning styles that sometimes occur between teachers and students. The solutions offered are practical and loving. This chapter might make teaching your children sound too hard, but don't let it intimidate you. Most of the time you will find that your lesson plan is fine and that your own interest and enthusiasm will carry the day. Homeschooling is a wonderful adventure, and this chapter will help you to get through some of the roadblocks in that adventure.

The interesting thing about learning styles is that when we become teachers, our learning style usually translates into our teaching style. For us to be the very best teachers possible for our own, specific, unique children, it is imperative that we understand why we do what we do. If not, we might expect to have headlong collisions with our children operating from a different learning style. These collisions certainly do not promote quality education!

Consider a thinker mom with an intuitor child. The mom has perfectly prepared, logically arranged, systematically organized lesson plans. Her intuitor daughter takes one look at mom's outline and suggests, "Hey, I know! Why don't we do _____ instead?" Mom glares at her student and replies, "Because this is the *right* way to do it, and it's all arranged. Now, sit down and get to work!" Do you see the potential for problems here? Unfortunately, the intuitor child's desire for spontaneity, ideas, and excitement may seem like rebellion to the thinker mother, though in reality they are part and parcel of the intuitor's style of learning.

How about a feeler mom with a thinker child? In the morning, Mom gets up and lovingly prepares her child's favorite breakfast. She is looking forward to sitting with her child on the couch to read a wonderful biography out loud. When her thinker child appears at the breakfast table, he asks what exactly is he expected to do this day? The mom says, "Well, I thought we could start that new biography on Hudson Taylor today and perhaps see how you are doing after we finish that." The thinker child replies in exasperation, "But Mom, I need to know what time we are going to start the book and how long it will take to read it. And what do you expect of me in this history project—do I need to write a report? How many pages? When is it due? Do I need a bibliography? If not a report, are you going to give me a test? What day? What kind of questions will you ask? How much time will I have to take the test?"

By this time, the feeler mom is completely unnerved; she hadn't expected to have to face all these questions before breakfast. She just wanted to sit together, have a pleasant meal, and then read together on the couch. By not understanding the differences between her needs for companionable relationship and her child's needs for organization, this feeler mom is heading for difficulty and frustration with her thinker child.

Such a collision occurs between any teacher and student. Each learning/teaching style has its strengths and its weaknesses. The collisions are caused when the contrasting strong points of a teacher and a learner don't mesh. To avoid these collisions, let's go through the teaching styles and take a look at mom as teacher.

⟞⟝ The mom with a thinker learning/teaching style will be very organized, structured, and orderly. She prefers a set routine with a dependable schedule—interruptions are not welcome. This mother will enjoy having a well-prepared lesson plan for each student, written in advance. If using textbooks, this mother will have adequately allowed time for their arrival before the first day of school, AND will have remembered to order the teacher's manual as well. The lessons will be set forth point by point in a reasonable, rational order.

These are all very wonderful qualities for a teacher to have *until* the student needs a bit of change and flexibility, the proverbial breath of fresh air. The thinker teacher needs to be aware of her own tendencies to organize and arrange to the nth degree, and to be careful not to stomp on her intuitor child's creative, spontaneous ideas. She must beware of being so planned out that the feeler child has no time for hugs, talking, or doing this part together. If the thinker mom's organizational, perfectionist tendencies are not brought under thoughtful control, she may prevent her sensor child from making messes and thereby learning through his senses. ("Junior, I told you to sit down and finish this workbook—NOW!")

Responding in love, the thinker mom will certainly prepare carefully, making sure all of the bases are covered, but she will be sensitive to know when her children need some flexibility.

⟞⟝ A mother with a feeler learning/teaching style will be most concerned about the intra-family relationships. Is everyone getting along with everyone else? Do all family members understand why they have their assignments? How do they all feel about their school? This mother will want to explain her plans and get everyone's feedback. As she plans out her schoolwork and schedule, she will be most anxious to show her students the people perspective in what they are studying. "What motivated Louis Pasteur to experiment with germs?" "How do people use algebra in real life?" "Learn to play this guitar so we can have family singalongs!"

The down side of this relation-oriented style is that sometimes a feeler mom can be easily manipulated once her students realize that she is paralyzed by disunity in the family. Your students may not like studying grammar or math, but they need to "take their medicine" like the rest of us and not just complain until they get Mom to cave in. As our earlier example demonstrates, a feeler mom with a thinker child needs to provide the child with enough structure and routine to satisfy his or her thinker tendencies; a feeler mom may get her feelings hurt when her intuitor child doesn't want to follow her lesson plan; a feeler mom feels left out when her project-oriented sensor child is too busy for a hug.

These responses will not offend a mother who remembers that they are in no way a reflection of her children's regard for her but are merely expressions of how the children approach a task. A loving response from the feeler mom would be to be strong enough for the children's sake to demand their best effort.

⟿ A sensor mom is the no-nonsense, practical, get-it-done kind of teacher. She will prefer the hands-on approach to teaching. This means that when the children need to study plant science, the sensor mom will get out the planters, potting soil, and seeds and commence studying in a practical way. She will enjoy teaching history if it incorporates making costumes and old-fashioned crafts, cooking, and model building, etc. This mom is a whirlwind, never-stop, bundle of energy and wows the rest of us with her stamina and ability.

The sensor mom, however, should work diligently to open the door for her children in the areas of books, ideas, discussions, and what might seem idle thought time. She needs to be aware of the needs of her children who have different learning styles. The thinker child may not *want* to plant seeds in dirty soil, preferring to look up the plant's life cycle in an encyclopedia. The feeler child may simply want to know, "Will it die?" and "Will you help me?" Mom, however, has no time for such impractical concerns. The intuitor child, again, will probably challenge Mom about how to plant the seeds, where to plant them, when to plant them, who should do the planting, and who should record the information.

⟿ The mom with an intuitor learning/teaching style usually has all kinds of ideas about teaching the various subjects. She prefers to create her own curriculum so that it fits the needs of her individual children. This mom loves spontaneity, breaks in routine, and keeping everyone guessing about what comes next. Rather than hating interruptions, she prays for them. She enjoys discussing ideas with her children and dreaming for the future. She can be a highly motivational teacher.

The difficulty for the intuitor mom, as I shared in my journal, is that she finds it very painful to follow through on her great ideas. She tends to avoid routine, and that can be disastrous for children, since they need a certain amount of routine for stability in their lives. The intuitor mom and a thinker child may feel as though they are speaking a foreign language not understood by the other. It is important, again, for the mom to recognize the needs of her thinker child and provide him with the order and routine he requires. When she is coming up with one of her great ideas, an intuitor mom with a feeler child may seem to neglect the child. Remember how an intuitor works very hard while sitting and looking out the window? A feeler child may not understand just what mom is doing and will feel left out of the process. A sensor child needs a practical, hands-on project to do now, while the intuitor mom avoids being practical whenever she can and certainly feels she can't perform these miracles on demand. Children quickly figure out that an intuitor mom can easily be led astray. All they have to do is ask questions and zoom! Away the intuitor mom goes, hurrying down all the rabbit trails you can imagine. (I had a professor like that in college—we'd get him talking about something entirely off the point, and he'd never get back to the original subject that entire day.)

To love her students, the intuitor mom needs to gather up her gumption to be organized, at least to some degree. Children benefit from dependable routine, and moms are the routine providers.

At this point, we need to address a critical aspect of teaching. I believe that we, as teachers, are to serve the needs of the students. In other words, the burden of the students' learning is upon US. This means it is not good enough to say, "Well, I had a fabulous lesson plan, all of the best books available, and a great idea for projects, so it's their own fault if they didn't learn anything." On the contrary, if the students didn't learn anything, the fault lies with the teacher and the methods for teaching that were employed.

Before you slump over in defeat, let me hasten to explain that this does not mean you have to have a degree in education to teach your own children. Homeschooling has been done for generations, and there are families all around you now who are doing extremely well. Many we have known with an education degree, in the schools and in the homes, have not accepted this responsibility and have failed to educate their students because they were not willing to become servants to the students. All teachers must accept this basic responsibility to serve their students by creating an opportunity for learning.

What does it mean to be a servant to the needs of your student? Basically, this concept implies that whatever it takes to communicate so that your children learn, you will do. If your sensor children cannot learn their multiplication tables while seated at a desk with a workbook, try something else. Let them do jumping jacks while repeating after you. Or have them walk up and down steps as they recite 2 x 2 = 4, 4 x 4 = 16, etc. If your thinker child cannot understand your wonderful idea for studying the action of the heart—"Everyone bring me a blue card that symbolizes oxygen-deficient blood coming to the heart through the veins, and I'll give you a red card that symbolizes oxygen-supplied blood returning to the body through the arteries"—then give him or her transparent flip charts, the science videos, and the best resources you can find on the subject. If your feeler child absolutely resists memorizing names, dates, and places in the history textbook, find a few fascinating biographies, some historical fiction, or some projects you can work on together and sit and talk about for a few minutes, and watch what happens!

This concept of being the servant means that if your best-laid plans are not giving your children what they need, scrap them and find something that better fits their learning style. When what is most important to you is the fact that your children truly learn something, the method of that learning becomes secondary. And as we'll see next, there are tried-and-true methods of teaching that respond to all the different learning styles.

The "All For One and One For All" Method

While reading through the excellent book *Learning Styles* by Marlene D. LeFever, I came across the concept of teaching our children using a cycle approach through all four learning styles. Though she uses different names for the four learning styles—imaginative (feeler), analytic (thinker), common sense (sensor), and dynamic (intuitor)—the author gives such clear examples that it is easy to understand the concept. LeFever has a gift for making a very difficult teaching concept simple.

She gives us a method to follow that includes lessons for all four learning styles.

How do we teach to all of the different learning styles? Does this mean endless lesson planning, overwhelming work, and ultimate failure for homeschool parents? No! No! No! We simply need to learn this technique for engaging all the learning styles and for getting each child motivated to learn.

A cycle, a pattern, a series of questions can help you understand how to engage and motivate your children. (This is my interpretation, my terminology of the excellent material contained in LeFever's book.) First, you need to grab 'em. Second, you need to teach 'em. Third, you need to apply 'em. Finally, you need to release 'em.

To grab 'em is to help them know the people perspective, the "Why are we studying this?" "Why is this important to know?" questions. It might be done through biographies, through historical fiction, through storytelling, or through your own explanation of how a particular subject was important in your life. This will engage the feeler in what is to be learned, though everyone will benefit from knowing the why. Remember, feelers are the people who need people! As feelers come to know about the benefit of this study, they will beam with pleasure and anticipation, and their eagerness will help everyone to look forward to what's coming next.

When you teach 'em, the thinker becomes engaged. This is the time of studying books, encyclopedias, charts, diagrams, the "facts, Ma'am, just the facts!" Obviously, everyone needs to know the facts, the charts, and the names, dates, and places. But this is where the thinker will thrive, and his/her enthusiasm for what is being learned will excite and motivate the rest of the family.

After you grab 'em and teach 'em, you must apply 'em. This is the practical, hands-on, here-and-now application of what your children have been studying. This is the domain of the sensor, the time where he/she will be able to "see the hill, take the hill!" This may involve doing crafts, building, cooking, gardening, measuring, gathering, hiking, and more, the primary focus being to move, involve the senses, and accomplish a project. Again, the sensor's excitement about finally getting to do something will be contagious for the rest of the family.

Finally, you need to release 'em. Your intuitors will jump to their feet at this point because this is the time of the "what if?", of creating something new out of what has been learned. When you release 'em, you allow them to soar to new heights, to "boldly go where no man has gone before." For an intuitor, there can be nothing more stimulating than having permission to dream up new ideas. And these new ideas will help all of the other family members to gain a fuller perspective of what has been learned.

Do you see the cycle? Grab 'em, teach 'em, apply 'em, and release 'em. Then start the cycle over again with the next area or phase of study. Let me hasten to assure you that you will probably spend days, perhaps weeks, in each part of the cycle, though I have found this four-part cycle to be of immense help even when I only had one hour to speak to a group of adults. It is possible to go through the entire cycle in that one hour.

Perhaps an example will clarify this concept. Suppose you decide that it is time for your children to study the Renaissance. You need to begin by gathering up your materials, resources, etc. and by considering this four-part cycle. How will you grab 'em? Whose story will you tell? What will you use to teach 'em? What maps, reprints, articles can you locate? What projects could be done to apply 'em? Which experiments, plays, projects can you attempt? How can you release 'em? What aspect needs more research or relates to interests your family has already? Be sure to give your children the basic game plan before you begin so that they will understand that an opportunity will be given during this study for their learning style to SHINE!

All right. To introduce the period of the Renaissance, you announce to your assembled children, "I have a few fabulous stories about people who lived during the time we call the Renaissance. For the next few days, after we finish math and language arts, I'm going to read these books out loud to give you a taste of what it was like to live back in that time. To finish off our introduction, when we complete the books, we are going to watch the movie *The Agony and the Ecstasy*, which is about Michelangelo painting the Sistine Chapel." The books you have chosen to read need to be appropriate to your children's age and interests, including some things they could read on their own. Perhaps you will want to use stories of Christopher Columbus, Johannes Kepler, Queen Elizabeth, Shakespeare, Galileo, Sir Francis Drake, the Spanish Armada, etc. (Refer to the wonderful resource book *The Timetables of History* to see all the possibilities of people and events to study.)

What a great introduction! Many people love to be read to, especially if the stories are exciting. Watching an appropriate movie can also be a treat and a wonderful visual aid to introduce a time period (the costumes and music are a tremendous boost!).

The week of introduction is over. Your children have a taste of the Renaissance and some of the important things that happened during that time. Your feeler is enthralled with the people he/she has met in books, and everyone is anticipating the next step. It is now time to teach 'em. Utilizing several books, textbooks, encyclopedias, maps, and charts, have your children begin to study the causes, the impact, the events of the Renaissance. In our family, we usually allow each child to pursue the particular area that interests him/her most, and the children report on their findings to the rest of us. You may, for example, have one child studying the artists of the Renaissance, another studying all the kings and queens and their offspring, still another investigating the exploration that was taking place (this was, after all, the Age of Explorers), and yet another wanting to study the scientific discoveries of that age. At the end of two or three weeks, all the family members gather to share what they have learned. This is learning through multiplication. Everyone's efforts are multiplied as each sees how his or her material is related to what the others were studying. Learning names, dates, places, and events will flow naturally in this phase. In fact, the thinker may decide to chart everyone's findings for clarification. This chart will also help to show the causes and effects of the Renaissance.

Now is the time to apply 'em. Suggest projects to illustrate the Renaissance and allow each child, again, to follow his or her interests. Some project ideas might include painting a picture while lying on your back (Michelangelo style), making a cardboard version of the Santa Maria (Columbus's sailing ship), building a set for your family's version of *Romeo and Juliet* (by Shakespeare), sewing costumes for the same play (Renaissance style), performing experiments with pendulums (a la Galileo), or setting up the battle of the Spanish Armada (with the coast of England made from playdough, ships constructed of Legos, and a tub of water with appropriate splashing for the incredible storms encountered). The sensors will especially appreciate this opportunity, perhaps even desiring to do several projects—but everyone, regardless of learning style, will grow in an understanding of the Renaissance as he or she participates.

Finally, it is time to release 'em. Ask your children such questions as, "How would you teach this subject to others?" or "What are the relationships between scientists and explorers and kings?" If you have an intuitor in your family, be prepared for the brainstorms. Your children might decide (under the prompting of the intuitor) to hold a Renaissance Evening for family and friends. The preparation time may require another few days, so be prepared. During this Renaissance Evening, music appropriate to the time will be played, food will be served that was familiar to the people who lived during that period, and the projects accomplished during the previous weeks will be displayed. Short descriptions of the important people of the Renaissance will be narrated by the children who enjoy talking to people. And perhaps the evening will conclude by enacting—whether in person or in puppetry—a short version of the Shakespearean play your children enjoyed reading most. (*Tales From Shakespeare* by Charles and Mary Lamb is a marvelous resource for this.)

It has taken perhaps two months to cycle through the subject of the Renaissance as you grab 'em, teach 'em, apply 'em, and release 'em. Do you see that with this understanding, you can engage each learning style? And when you engage your children, it will motivate them to learn. At each stage, you will introduce your children to the material and then facilitate their growth in learning. This cycle works for every subject, for adults as well as for children. It adds the dynamic of interest and enthusiasm for each learning style and prevents your school from being caught in a rut.

This cycle will enable you to reach and motivate all your children. It is very good for all of us to be exposed to others' best style of learning—it brings growth and expansion to our understanding. The cross-fertilization factor of learning material in four different ways will also mean that your children will assimilate far more learning than they would have in a conventional or one-dimensional setting.

If you are feeling overwhelmed at this point, relax. My suggestion to you is to try the grab 'em – teach 'em – apply 'em – release 'em system in a small way. Get your feet wet with a four-day lesson before you try swimming for four weeks. Allow this concept to develop in your home over a period of time until it becomes second nature to you. Believe me, your children will want to help you to implement this, since it will allow for such variety in their one-room schoolhouse.

Recommended Reading

Learning Styles by Marlene D. LeFever
    The best book I've read about how to teach to the different learning styles. Though the author is primarily addressing Sunday school teachers, her principles and examples are very useful to homeschoolers.

Learning Styles and Tools by Alta Vista
    Very easy to follow, written for homeschooling parents, the book describes the four learning styles discussed in this chapter. Included are tests for determining learning styles and helpful suggestions for teaching each style.

The Way They Learn by Cynthia Ulrich Tobias
    Probably the most enjoyable to read book on learning styles, Cynthia's presentation is loaded with humorous examples. Not only does she explain the four learning styles (using different terms than I used), she also describes modalities, different environments for learning, and the seven intelligences.

People Types and Tiger Stripes by Gordon Lawrence
    A summary of the concepts developed during Meyers-Briggs's extensive research. Not easy reading, since it is very analytical, with extensive detail. However, you will find it to be invaluable for an in-depth understanding of this subject. It is currently being applied in management/employee evaluations.

The Seven Laws of the Learner by Dr. Bruce Wilkinson
    The subtitle of this book is "How to Teach Almost Anything to Practically Anyone!" and that is exactly what it teaches you. One of the most valuable books I've ever read for demonstrating the various techniques a teacher can utilize to convey information to his/her students. Invaluable!

Chapter 8

〰️

The One-Room Schoolhouse
Multilevel Teaching

*O*ne splendid September day, we had the opportunity to tour a museum in Maine with our friends, the Delacruz family. The museum itself was a fascinating collection of memorabilia—from books to threshers—concerning the history of this Maine village. Since it was then the off-season, one of the museum volunteers came and "interpreted" the museum for us. This dear, elderly lady was a distant relation to Clara Barton, which made her very special to our daughter.

When we had finished touring all the displays, our museum interpreter asked if we would be interested in seeing the one-room schoolhouse that had been recently moved to the museum grounds. Though the skies were now threatening a downpour, we all jumped at the chance to see this historic educational building. As we dodged raindrops and then eagerly dashed into the welcoming shelter, our guide told us that she had actually been a teacher in this school building. How her eyes shone as she described the daily routine, especially during the winter.

Both of us homeschool moms were singularly encouraged in our mission of educating our own children. Though there were certainly differences between this historic school and our present-day homeschools, it was heartening to meet someone who had successfully and cheerfully

119

taught several different grade levels every day in the same room. In fact, the obvious joy of her memories was a foretaste of what our rewards will be.

Our Journal

In 1992, we moved back to Bill's home state of South Dakota. We had been planning to make the change from Washington but were hastened along when Bill's widowed mother broke her foot. Because she was alone and unable to get around easily, our coming was a blessing to her as well as to us.

We moved from a three-thousand-square-foot house into three bedrooms in the second story of her Victorian-style home. Wwhhhhppppffff! "The incredible shrinking space!" and "Honey, I shrunk the living quarters!" describe the sensation. Though it was grand to be with Bill's mom, it was an adjustment for us all, especially when it came to school.

Back in Washington we had enjoyed a tremendous amount of space for school, lots of bookshelves full of homeschooling titles, an art cupboard teeming with artsy things, a couch to snuggle on while reading books out loud, and lots of rumble room for growing children. In South Dakota, since we wanted to keep our schoolroom separate from where my mother-in-law was recovering, we had one small bookcase with our most-needed books and my bed for school. And that was it!

Do you know, it was the best year of school we had ever had? I believe it was due mainly to our one-room (literally!) schoolhouse. We had no choice but to study most of our subjects together, and the wonderful discussions and brainstorming that resulted made school an exciting place to be. When we studied world history, for example, one child would ask a question, and pretty soon we would all have different books—my study Bible, a timeline, an encyclopedia, and *Timetables of History*—opened up on the bed. We would spend hours searching out information, tracing civilizations, and seeing God's amazing plan revealed. (That was the beginning of my seminar *What in the World's Going On Here?*)

As we worked through science together, as we discussed world history, as we read out loud from classic literature, something very special happened. We began to know each other in a new way, and we discovered each person's unique strengths and interests. We became friends like we had never been before *because we were together even in our studies.*

God is so good! We believe that it was His goodness to us that brought us hurriedly from the West Coast so that we might experience our special one-room schoolhouse for that one year. We learned far more than had been our normal schoolyear experience, because we were working together to learn. We forged friendships with one another in our tiny living space that have deepened through the years, directly traceable to that moment in our family's history. Oh, and Bill's mom recovered.

A Meeting of the Minds

How does one teach in a one-room schoolhouse setting at home? Is every subject adaptable to being learned *en masse*? Can children several years apart in age actually learn together? Does it really work?

First of all, though you may have never experienced learning in a one-room schoolhouse, it was the primary model for school throughout much of our country's history. As far as I can tell, those students had a tremendously successful education and learned far more than most students in school settings today. (Yes, of course, the standards and practices in education have also made a significant difference. I am just trying to point out that it didn't *hurt* a child to be taught in such a setting.)

Have you read any old books that in passing describe the dynamics of a one-room schoolhouse? Books such as Laura Ingalls Wilder's *These Happy Golden Years* are a treasure trove of encouragement for us. These oldtime authors described the mechanics of teaching several different ages at the same time. Though there were different levels of achievement, each group was aware of the lessons of the others. Spelling bees, geography bees, literary evenings, singing school, and more, all incorporated everyone present. There were opportunities to discuss topics all together, to learn new information with everyone involved. Younger children learned from the older children's lessons; older children received refresher courses when listening to the younger children. And the older children were often called upon to help with the younger children's studies. (Recall who learns the most about a subject—the teacher!) Even though there was a diversity of ages, there was a sense of being one class. Everyone benefited in various ways from the interaction between the ages.

It has been done and can be done, and perhaps can even benefit from a new twist. Now, how do you do it? What subjects are adaptable to being learned, albeit on different levels of understanding, by all of your school-ready children at one time? (We'll talk about toddlers later.) Is this really a back-door approach to get you into unit studies? No, not really. You can use a traditional approach in a one-room schoolhouse—teachers did it successfully for years. But it does work quite nicely with unit studies as well.

Let's consider first the subjects that require special one-on-one attention, for they will be more difficult to fit into an all-together style of learning session. The three Rs will be the most likely subjects to teach separately and individually. Beginning readers will need a lot of instruction in phonics to build a sound base for reading. If you have more than one beginner, you can certainly teach them at the same time, but basic phonics will probably not be interesting to your junior high level reader. It would be wise, however, to occasionally have your junior high student help your beginner.

Beginning readers also need practice in reading out loud, which provides an excellent opportunity for older students to be involved. And don't limit your beginner to Dick and Jane stories. There are wonderful books, such as the Christian Liberty Press beginner reading series, that cover real topics—history, science, famous people—instead of fluff.

Spelling, the handmaiden of phonics, is usually taught separately. This year, however, I am taking all of my children through the same books, *Writing Road to Reading* and *Teaching Reading at Home*, to make sure their foundation in spelling is secure. It has worked well for us, since my children are all advanced readers. You might have to teach two separate spelling classes, as we did last year—one for your beginners and one for your advanced students—if you want to utilize these excellent materials.

Penmanship can be taught either individually or corporately. Since I had put off teaching cursive to Michael and Melody for a few years, it was appropriate to teach them together. Actually, I thought a refresher course for Isaac wouldn't hurt, so all three went through a daily class of penmanship for about three months. The results were worth it; their penmanship improved considerably, and they acquired an enjoyment of writing by hand (the computer is still the instrument of choice, however).

Math is usually an individual subject, as it progresses sequentially year by year. However, if your family plays math games (like Cathy Duffy's *Math Mouse*), practices math facts, or learns principles of algebra when building a playhouse, it will be able to share that mathematical learning experience.

Bear in mind that though the three Rs will be the most likely subjects to teach separately and individually, you can still incorporate all your students at their various levels by (1) having your older students occasionally sit in on some of your beginners' classes for a refresher course, (2) teaching your advanced students how to help the beginners in their studies, and (3) incorporating the three Rs into your other subjects, such as reading for your science class and writing reports for your history class.

What subjects *are* easily adaptable for a multilevel approach? Though not an exhaustive list, we have found that the Bible, history, science, literature, economics, music, art, and physical education are all suitable for learning together. Admittedly, if you also have little ones, this will be a challenge to your ingenuity and adaptability. Some suggestions and ideas will be offered later in this chapter about this.

Here are some ideas for teaching these subjects to all (or several) of your children at once:

☙ When it comes to history and science, it is not as important which year you teach what as it is that your students receive all of it eventually. Hence, you could teach your state's history to your fourth, fifth, and sixth grader in the same year, though the local public school may do it during the fifth grade year. I know of homeschool moms who have two or three children close in age, and they simply use the same books in history or science for their group, saving time *and* money. These moms assign projects, written reports, experiments, etc., for the children in that group. The assignments are often made somewhat longer or more difficult for the older student. Again, this could be within either a traditional or a unit study approach.

☙ Another wonderful, stimulating way to expose your entire family to multilevel learning is by reading good books out loud. Through them you may learn about history, science, politics, inventions, explorations, and discoveries as well as good literature. The shared experience of reading out loud is one of the best ways of making knowledge available to each one in the family on his or her own level. For instance, in our family, we read *Penny Candy* by Richard Maybury for the introduction to our study of economics. Bill and I, as adults, learned the information on one level, while Melody, our 10-year-old, learned it on a different level. But now we all have a working understanding of the concepts of supply and demand, inflation and recession, velocity of money, etc. As Melody matures, her understanding of these concepts will mature. (As our resident thinker, her understanding of economics probably is beyond ours anyway.)

⚘ Games are a fabulous means for learning together. Whether you want to study math, Greek and Latin roots, history, geography, spelling, vocabulary, the Bible, art, music, or Shakespeare, wonderful educational games are available. We have become believers in utilizing this tool as we've seen our children learn effortlessly in the course of playing a game. We have many family nights of educational game playing, and even assign games during school from time to time. From youngest to oldest, we have found educational games to be a tremendous boost to our learning.

Some of our favorite educational games: Rummy Roots (Greek and Latin roots), The Play's the Thing (Shakespeare), Made for Trade (colonial life), Mankala (an African counting game), Boggle (vocabulary/ spelling), Scrabble (vocabulary/spelling), Mastermind (logic), and Axis and Allies (WWII history). We also have picked up many games that are no longer available but are treasures to our family. Look through *your* game closet and see what might breathe new life into a school subject!

⚘ Don't forget the impact of discussions over the dinner table about an educational/informational subject. This is a tremendous time of learning for everyone whether you discuss evolution vs. creation, *Anne of Green Gables*, or the principle of tithing. Discussions allow knowledge to be shared with one another in an informal, open-forum setting. Our children often come up with the most marvelous questions, which start the discussion ball rolling. We've discussed everything from astronauts to ziggurats over dinner, often with my running for the encyclopedia to give the final word.

If your family is not very comfortable (yet!) with discussions, talk it over with your spouse. Together, plan out some possible topics for discussion that would be appropriate for your children. Then, at the next opportunity, gently bring the topic into the conversation. Ask your children what they think about _____ or how they would have done differently or why someone would be interested in doing_____, etc. Believe me, you don't need to be a rocket scientist to have discussions with your children.

⚘ Projects are one of the most popular all-together learning times for us. As we all work on the same project or on similar projects at the same time, we build a feeling of camaraderie and sharing in our learning.

At our house, we have found it very motivating to plan an evening when everyone's project will be displayed, artwork hung, skits and puppet shows performed, science experiments conducted, etc., AND when friends and family will be invited to come—a sort of Gala Homeschool Presentation Night. When one faces a deadline for performance, it helps to stimulate one's efforts!!! (As we saw in the chapter on learning styles, however, some of us are stimulated and motivated only at the last moment!)

Projects offer our students a chance to inform each other and to share with each other what they have been learning, which is another opportunity for "cross-fertilization." It is amazing how much more we can learn and how much more interesting a presentation can be when the students have already been involved and have shared answers, ideas, etc., during preparation.

We experienced this marvelous cross-fertilization one winter as we studied astronomy together. To introduce this subject from a creationist point of view, Bill and I read out loud from an intriguing book, *Astronomy and the Bible* by Donald DeYoung. We read exciting biographies of early astronomers like Johannes Kepler and Galileo. Our family also studied books on stars, planets, galaxies, and more, which we checked out of our local library. We had an astronomy lab several evenings a week (whenever the temperature was above zero!), where each child had an individualized lab with our telescope, searching the night skies for items of interest.

To immerse them in some aspect of astronomy, we asked our children what specific area interested them enough to produce a project. After some discussion and thought, Isaac decided he would like to study the big bang theory from the contrasting viewpoints of evolution and creation. Michael, who had recently read *Carry On, Mr. Bowditch* (concerning Nathanial Bowditch, the father of the modern navigational tables), thought that it would be very intriguing to learn about how sailors used the stars for navigation. Melody, after great consideration, settled on the discovery in the early 1900s of the planet Pluto. As you can imagine, each of our children was studying and preparing for a project quite different from the others.

The night of our homeschool presentation, we settled back to watch the results of all their hard work. Isaac had chosen to verbally explain, along with a written report, the reasoning behind the big bang theory, carefully pointing out the faulty logic and irrational thinking that contributed to the evolutionists' point of view—using their own words! Michael had several illustrations of the use of a sextant in determining latitude and longitude, and a description of the sailor's thorough knowledge of the heavens—"I know it like the back of my hand!" (He still helps me find the various constellations; they don't all look the same to *him*!) Melody, with the help of a fellow puppeteer, chose to describe, with a puppet skit, Pluto and its discovery. Before the presentation, she had prepared the ceiling to show Pluto's unusual orbit around the sun by hanging mini-planets on string. As Melody described for us how Pluto's orbit was sometimes outside Neptune's (thus being the most distant planet) and sometimes inside Neptune's (thus being the second most distant planet), I was flabbergasted! I had gone to school! I had learned about the planets! Why did I have to wait until my late thirties to learn *this*???? (Again, one of the great benefits of homeschooling is getting to learn all those things that either you never heard or you heard but have forgotten!)

The cross-fertilization occurred for us all that night as we each learned something new from the presenters. Many references have since been made to the information learned that night, which demonstrate that knowledge was truly acquired and that the issues raised (especially about creation vs. evolution) are still being pursued.

All of the above points are doable to some degree in every family. Read fascinating books out loud, play exciting educational games, hold lively discussions, and work on stimulating, creative projects together. Whether you prefer a traditional curriculum, a teachable moment approach, or a unit study curriculum, your family can benefit tremendously from these kinds of interaction, of being a one-room schoolhouse at home.

What About the Wee Ones?

Though certainly no expert on teaching with preschoolers at home, I will share with you my own limited experiences and what other, more experienced homeschooling moms have shared with me. From listening to homeschoolers all over the country I have come to believe that with God's help, *anything*—including schooling with wee ones—is possible.

Probably the most important concept to keep in mind is that our homeschools are not static, not unchanging. Every year will be a new year, with different dynamics, different possibilities, different levels of capability, and different external circumstances. So...relax! If you are struggling with the impossibilities facing you this year, don't give up. Your experience each year makes the subsequent year smoother.

Secondly, in the midst of relaxing, pray (I believe the qualifiers here would be "fervently" and "unceasingly"). Ask God for His wisdom, His strength, His patience, His kindness, and His compassion in your situation. Remember, "Ask and you shall receive, seek and you shall find, knock and the door shall be opened to you" (Matthew 7:7, Luke 11:9). Trust that God will make a way where there seems to be no way. The longer we have homeschooled, the more we have seen that God Himself is in the midst of our family, our children's education, and our direction. It is a sure and certain fact that God cares about your homeschool and will help you—so just ask.

Now for the practical considerations. Depending on their ages and their siblings, you can structure your school around the little one's nap time, appoint an older sibling to read to/play with the youngest while Mom works with another student, plug in a good children's video (such as *The Amazing Book!*)—though I would counsel you to limit this considerably, provide preschool "schoolbooks" or activities that the younger children can work on while the older children do their schoolwork (good for varying periods of time). If your little ones are old enough, try using *5 In a Row* with them for thirty minutes to an hour each day. They will have had their own "school" and may be content to share Mom with the other students.

Another suggestion that has been shared with me is to use your computer. Look for some of the preschool educational software programs available. One mother I know absolutely swears by them. Her young ones have learned many things through the computer (shapes, colors, numbers, etc.), and their enthrallment with the computer has given her a free hour here and there to work exclusively with her older children.

These are a mere handful of ideas for schooling with wee ones. If you are struggling in this area and these suggestions are not sufficient, let me encourage you to find a homeschool support group in your area. Talk to the other moms until you find someone who has worked or is working through this area also. Perhaps you can trade babysitting a few days a week to free up time to accomplish the most demanding teaching for your older children. Perhaps this other mom has discovered the absolute, surefire, proven solution to loving your very young children while overseeing your older ones. Perhaps her husband will talk to your husband and explain the importance of Dad's taking charge of the wee ones while Mom teaches the older ones at night. Or vice versa. Maybe what you need is some uninterrupted time of snuggling down with your little ones at night. That might entirely change your attitude during the schoolday. The most important aspect of this would be that someone else can walk with you, encourage you, and pray with you about the needs of your homeschool. And that is the best solution I know.

The Family That Studies Together
Should Also Work Together

Face it. The second law of thermodynamics is true. In lay terms, the second law of thermodynamics says that things will go from a state of order to a state of increasing disorder unless energy is applied. And I can prove it! Just visit my house for an entire day and watch it grow messier and messier, more and more disorganized until someone applies force to the situation, that someone usually being me.

How does this apply to homeschooling? It means that we need to be aware of this law of thermodynamics and take steps to prevent it from disorganizing our homes and lives. It means that we need an organized plan for dealing with disorganized messes. For homeschoolers, this plan needs to involve your children as well.

At one point in our homeschooling life, I was totally overwhelmed and ready to throw in the towel. I was the wife, the mom, the nurse, the cook, the laundress, the chauffeur, the bookkeeper, the teacher, the sergeant-at-arms, and the police detective ("Who made this mess?"). In talking the situation over with Bill, I realized that much of the burden would be removed from me if I could give up the sergeant-at-arms and the police detective roles. It was very difficult to be the loving, nurturing, listening, caring, creative mom while having to enforce the performance of chores by unwilling, complaining children. (Oops! Was I not supposed to mention that part?) I think my children were unwilling and complaining because I was always so uptight about getting the chores done...not a nice person. So it was with tremendous relief that I relinquished that part of my job description to Bill. And my children were wonderfully blessed in the process.

Bill, the detail person in our marriage, carefully looked through several materials we had relating to how to get your kids to help with chores. He set up a rotating schedule for the five of us which has worked wonderfully for the past several years. This year he added cooking and laundry to the list: each child has his/her own day for doing laundry, and each child is responsible for one breakfast, one lunch, and one dinner per week.

Since I have three children, that makes nine meals I don't have to plan, cook, or clean up after. Oh, the joy! Oh, the freedom! And oh, how much my children are learning about the realities and creativities of cooking! I kept wondering how on earth to teach my children about the different aspects of cooking, about preparing nutritionally sound, beautifully prepared, and aesthetically served food. As they have been assigned these three meals per week, I have encouraged them to scour my cookbooks, look through ethnic cookbooks at the library, and discover new old family favorites. Because of the emphasis on ethnic cooking, we may have a Russian breakfast, an English lunch, and an Italian dinner—all on the same day. But the children are motivated to learn, since they get to choose (within reason) what they are going to cook. This does not require any extra preparation or setup, since you would be there working at this time anyway. One caution I have discovered: Be prepared to come to the rescue if it is the first time a dish has been prepared by that child.

We have had wonderful discussions about appropriate side dishes, desserts, salads, soups, and breads. My children are all learning to use our new bread machine, so if I need help, I can say, "Who wants to make the cinnamon rolls for tomorrow?" or "Who has time to make French bread for tonight?" My children are all collecting their favorite recipes, favorite breakfast foods, favorite soups, and favorite main courses. They are learning to prepare Mexican, Russian, Italian, English, Middle Eastern, and good old American dishes. What a delight it has been, what a confidence builder for the future, all because Bill so wisely added this "chore" to their list of things to do.

Though I know each family has different ages, different requirements, and different needs, we all have things in common. We all need to eat (which requires cooking, setting the table, clearing the table, and washing the dishes), we all need to sleep (which should require making the beds daily), we all need to be clean (which means bathing, brushing hair and teeth, washing hands and face), we all need to be able to move through our homes without tripping (which means hanging up clothes, putting away books, storing toys, picking up papers, etc.), we all need to be able to breathe without fear of contamination (which means dusting, vacuuming, mopping, sweeping, cleaning the bathroom), and we all need to wear clothes (which means washing, drying, folding, mending, and ironing). With that in mind, and because our plan may inspire your own plan, we present:

The Waring Family Chore Chart

Melody's Schedule

Monday	Tuesday	Wednesday	Thursday	Friday	Saturday
_____	Lunch	Laundry	Dinner	Breakfast	_____
Bathroom	_____	Garbage	_____	Vacuum	Dust
Unload Dishwasher	Handwash Dishes	Set Table Helper	Unload Dishwasher	Clear Table	Set Table Helper

Michael's Schedule

Monday	Tuesday	Wednesday	Thursday	Friday	Saturday
Laundry	Breakfast	Dinner	Lunch	_____	_____
Garbage	_____	Vacuum	Dust	Bathroom	_____
Clear Table	Set Table Helper	Unload Dishwasher	Set Table Helper	Unload Dishwasher	Handwash Dishes

Isaac's Schedule

Monday	Tuesday	Wednesday	Thursday	Friday	Saturday
Laundry	Dinner	Lunch	Breakfast	_____	_____
Vacuum	Dust	Bathroom	_____	Garbage	_____
Set Table Helper	Unload Dishwasher	Clear Table	Handwash Dishes	Set Table Helper	Clear Table

(Hey, folks, it ain't much, but it works for now!)

A one-room schoolhouse at home includes studying together, reading together, working together, eating together, laughing together, praying together…living together. It requires organization and spontaneity, creativity and a familiar structure, warmth and discipline. May yours flourish!

Recommended Reading

Lessons From History by Gail Schultz
A wonderful set of three volumes that allow you to study history as a family. Gail includes suggestions of great books to read (on several different levels), discussion questions and projects, as well as a brief description of the people or events of an era.

Visual Manna (an art curriculum) by Richard and Sharon Jeffus
A curriculum encompassing all aspects of art and all grade levels. This one is especially appreciated because it includes both younger student activities as well as older student activities for each concept of art.

Is There Life After Housework? by Don Aslett
This is our "textbook" for cleaning the house. Because it is so humorously written, there is a constant clamor to study it.

Tracking Your Walk by Jim and Michelle Drake
This wonderful book is a children's prayer journal. (You need one for each child.) Because this is a creative and interesting format, it is an excellent tool to draw all of your children into penmanship, creative writing, geography, history, missions, Bible study, and prayer.

Chapter 9

⊙◍◍◍☉

If I Can't Draw a Stick Man, How Do I Teach Art?
and Other Important Questions

*I*n the days before homeschool art programs, such as *Visual Manna* and *How Great Thou ART*, allowed us to teach art as a normal, standard part of our week, I received a call. My friend Patty telephoned to invite my children and me over for lunch. She sounded so eager, fairly bursting with enthusiasm, when she said they had a show-and-tell from their homeschool that morning. Since Patty's children, Tiffany and Timothy, were good friends of my children, we were all excited to accept this unexpected invitation.

When we arrived, Patty led us over to the dining room table. "Look at these!" she rejoiced triumphantly. Beautiful illustrations, well-drawn and wonderfully colored, covered the table. All three of them had the results of the day's art lesson on display.

"Wow, Patty! I didn't know you could draw like this!"

I was impressed! But not nearly as much as when she showed me the drawings they had made before their lesson. The before drawings resembled my own untrained, untalented "works of art." The after drawings were amazingly well-proportioned, with correct perspective, very life-like, and beautiful.

Patty pulled out the book that had transformed their drawing skills,

Drawing with Children. "It's all in here!" she eagerly exclaimed. Though she was quick to point out the improvements made by her children, it was obvious that Patty was also very excited about her own development in art. I was astounded that a normal homeschooling mom, a regular nonartist type of person could learn so much from a book *and* could teach her children how to create art from a book.

Our Journal

All was quiet on the homeschool front. Life was progressing steadily, times were good, when all of a sudden, Michael asked me an impossible question.

"Mom, why do steel ships float?" I frantically searched the area, looking wild-eyed all around me, but having moved our residence to South Dakota, there was not a single steel ship (nor even a large body of water) in sight.

"I don't have a clue, but now that you mention it, I've always kind of wondered about that myself."

Knowing what every good homeschool mom knows—when in doubt, go to the library—I bundled up the children, and we walked to our local library to search out the answer to this impossible question.

We corralled our librarian, Pat, and put the question to her. She puzzled thoughtfully for a few moments and then raced off to find the appropriate books. Unfortunately for me, the only books she could find were beyond my reach, being books on the design and engineering of boats, and much too technical for my understanding.

I didn't know the answer, and the library couldn't inform me (in a language I spoke!). Where else could I turn? My husband and I began to scour the reference books tucked away around the house. Still, we could find nothing that explained why *steel* ships floated.

Two weeks after the impossible question was asked, we were sitting in our room discussing the difficulties we were having in coming up with an answer. Suddenly, I leapt across the room to grab a book we had not yet considered, *How in the World*, by Reader's Digest. Hoping against hope that the book would contain some reference to Michael's query, we looked in the index. Believe it or not, there was the listing: "steel ship buoyancy." With a jubilant yell, we turned to the article entitled "Why Do Steel Ships Float?" The first paragraphs in this particularly pertinent portion described the Greek mathematician Archimedes, who discovered the principle of buoyancy.

As Archimedes would have said—Eureka! We, who had no degrees in engineering, mathematics, science, or steel shipping(!), were able to satisfactorily answer Michael's impossible question, which led us to a study of the Greeks, of Archimedes and his war machines, and of the science of buoyancy and then to the laboratory. Michael devised an experiment to demonstrate the relationship between an object's shape and its corresponding displacement of water, which is the principle of buoyancy, which is why steel ships float.

Q. *How do I teach art to my children when I can't even draw a stick man? And is it important enough to bother with anyway?*

A. The second question needs to be answered first. Though most of us receive a very limited exposure to art in school (my main memory was of fingerpainting), we need to not neglect this subject in our homeschools. To be familiar with the great masterpieces of art, to understand what the artists are trying to communicate, to be aware of the amazing skill and techniques of these artists, to comprehend the worldview behind each painting, and to be equipped to communicate, even in a limited fashion, through this medium are all part and parcel of being a well-educated Christian. (You mean homeschooler? No, I mean Christian, whether homeschooler or otherwise.)

Down through the ages, art has been used both to express worship to God and to communicate ideas to man. Understanding art, and especially the ideas/worldviews the artist is trying to portray, can help train our children to be effective "bridge builders," better able to communicate to a lost and dying world. If you look at a Picasso and say, "This is crazy! Why couldn't this guy paint things so I can understand what they are?", without pressing on to understand just *why* Picasso painted in a disjointed, splintered, abstract manner, you will miss a vital link in understanding this vivid expression of the hopelessness and confusion of modern man. And if we don't understand this hopelessness, we will not be adept at communicating the hope that lies within us.

Furthermore, if our children are gifted by God in this area, they will learn to communicate true worship to God and express His loving care to the world through various types of art forms. Through their work, non-Christians will be impacted dramatically. A true story illustrating a nonbeliever's life having been changed by an artistic expression is that of my friend Judy Sample. Judy had had a brief encounter with Jesus Christ as a youth, but having had no discipling, she turned away with a vengeance from following the Lord.

In her 20s she was living in Rotterdam, Holland, utterly immersed in the arts, teaching teachers and students about music and movement. However, the type of art Judy taught was the avant garde style of art, which seeks to destroy, is completely negative, and is often occultic (the kind of stuff that we wouldn't even think of seeing). During a vacation in Europe, Judy decided to take a personal art tour to see many of the wonderful works of master artists throughout the centuries. As an artist herself, she held a tremendous appreciation for the talent and expression she saw in these paintings, regardless of the content.

While at the Komar Museum in France, she studied a series of paintings by Grunewald (1470–1528). These paintings from the Ishenheim altar were of the death and resurrection of Christ. The first painting she came to was of the crucifixion. As she stared long and hard at the artwork, she realized that the corpse of Jesus was really *dead*—it was true that Jesus had really died, in real history. That was the beginning of the awakening in her spirit, but when she walked around to see the other panel, she saw Grunewald's depiction of the resurrection. It was suddenly revealed to her that the resurrection actually happened—it was true, also. Jesus had been resurrected, He was alive, this was an actual, glorious event! It changed her whole life, putting her back on the path of walking with the Lord, which resulted in her husband Chris being converted as well.

Today, Judy is still an artist, but a redeemed one. God did not take away her art; He *fulfilled* it. Judy now works with homeschoolers, doing unit studies on dance and music, expressing the godliness of early colonial families in the eighteenth century. Doesn't that sound amazing? Judy is freer now as a redeemed artist to express the gifting God has placed inside her than she had been when she pursued a worldview of hopelessness and despair.

Can you imagine the scene in heaven when Judy thanks Grunewald for painting those pictures? Can you picture the absolute *joy* of this man to know that his artistic expression of truth actually brought someone into the Kingdom? And can you see the validity of encouraging our budding artists to paint to the glory of God?

If we, as parents, are not artists, how on earth do we teach these things to our children? Good question! Fortunately, when we homeschool today, we need not be limited by what we ourselves do not know.

If you missed the course in high school, didn't understand the material in class, never could find anyone who explained it clearly, you can still bring it to your children. Tremendous resources are available to help homeschoolers give their children an excellent education, regardless of their specific interests, while teaching them information they may have forgotten or never learned. [Diana's maxim for homeschoolers: The sky's the limit!]

For art, there are books, curriculums, computer software programs, videos, and materials readily available to your homeschool. If you prefer outside help, ask the local librarian, the 4-H leader, or possibly the local school district. You may find some excellent art programs that your children can access. (Just be sure to check out the program and the instructor carefully.)

To thoroughly teach art, the two parts to consider are art history/appreciation and how to do it yourself. To become an appreciative, knowledgeable audience, we need to understand something about art history—the masterpieces of art and the artists who created them, the development and techniques of art. In addition, everyone should have some basic instruction in the elements of drawing so that they do not end up art illiterates, not able to draw anything more than stick men. Take those who show an interest beyond the basics of drawing into the wonderfully creative world of oils, pastels, watercolors, charcoals, pen and ink, etc.

Wonderful resources are available for teaching art history/appreciation. If you are not familiar with Dr. Francis Schaeffer's *How Should We Then Live?*, I suggest you rent the video and watch the unfolding of humanist worldviews and the contrasting expressions of a Christian worldview through historic masterpieces of art. Junior high/senior high students would also profit from watching the video and studying the book with you.

From this same perspective, Cornerstone Curriculum Project offers a marvelous art history program called *Adventures in Art*, suitable for elementary and above. This is a three-year program, with museum-quality reproductions of art masterpieces arranged to show the Christian worldview contrasted to the development of the humanist worldview. We consider this program one of the priceless additions to our homeschooling endeavor and highly recommend it for everyone. For an overview of art history, Usborne's *Story of Painting* is good. A far more thorough senior high/college level text is Janson's *History of Art*. There will probably be several more art history books available in your local library, but be aware that most are not fit for childlike consumption.

If you have the opportunity to visit art museums that display historic masterpieces, by all means do so. One spring we visited Duluth, Minnesota, and learned that the university had an art museum with a European section. What a fabulous time! We walked our children through the historic European section first, then through the early American section, and ended our visit in the modern art section. It was so obvious to all of us, even seven-year-old Melody, that the ideas of what to paint, why to paint, and how to paint had changed drastically through the years. (If you have the chance, go through the museum before you take your younger children. There may be some paintings you want to avoid, especially in the modern section.)

How do you teach your children the basics of drawing? There are many good books available on the market. Our first art instruction book was very inexpensive, *very* helpful, and very usable for teaching ages six through adult. *The Drawing Textbook* by Bruce McIntyre shows the student how to draw, utilizing the elements of perspective: surface, size, surface lines, overlapping, shading, density, and foreshortening. The author teaches each of these elements in small increments while giving the student simple to increasingly complex objects to draw that will develop that particular skill. Isaac and I went through the book together, and while I did not continue to practice—having been very content to simply draw a good picture of Mickey Mouse—Isaac has progressed very quickly and has become very skillful in handling perspective.

Another excellent book for teaching drawing is *Drawing with Children* by Mona Brookes. The aspect of drawing learned in this book are the five basic elements of shape: the dot family, circle family, straight-line family, curved-line family, and angle-line family. The book presents some excellent ideas for becoming familiar with these shapes and for becoming comfortable in using them.

A new art curriculum written especially for Christian homeschoolers is called *Visual Manna's Complete Art Curriculum* for grades 1–12. Produced by an artist and an art teacher, Richard and Sharon Jeffus, this is a well-thought-out, well-conceived, and wonderfully executed program. I especially appreciate the Learning Expectations listed at the front of the book, as it tells you and your students exactly what is to be learned. This program covers such topics as calligraphy, sculpture, papier-mâché, perspective, illustrating books, weaving, animation and video, printing, and more. Included also are several masterpieces of art with brief introductions to the paintings.

From the company, How Great Thou ART, Barry Stebbing, another wonderful artist, has developed several different materials for teaching drawing, painting, shading, and many other techniques. As you might have guessed from the company's name, Mr. Stebbing's materials are geared specifically for Christians. We have heard absolutely fabulous reports from homeschooling families using these materials.

With all of these wonderful resources (and the many more I have not mentioned), what is left to do? Begin right now by hanging a master-piece on your wall, observing it, studying it, discussing it, copying it, and learning from it. Begin also right now to draw, to illustrate, to cartoon—however imperfectly—and allow this God-given ability to develop in you and your students. The sky's the limit!

Q. *I always slept through history class because it was so boring. How am I supposed to teach it to my children?*

A. Since history is one of my passions, I've worked hard to make it vivid and stimulating for my children. Here are some lessons I learned about teaching sit-on-the-edge-of-your-chair-in-suspense history.

The first thing children need is to discover the *fascination* of history, that we can have a front-row seat to view the most amazing events that ever happened, the most interesting people who ever lived, and the incredible way God works His perfectly timed will in history. Talk enthu-siastically to your children about history, about what God does in his-tory. If you don't know these things yourself, you have the fabulous opportunity to learn right along with your children!

The second important concept is to teach the *flow* of history, the big picture, the overview. You see, to the question, Which came first, the Greeks or the Romans…and could it possibly matter?, there is a resound-ingly important answer that affects even the birth of Jesus Christ. Do you remember during what empire Jesus lived, died, and was resurrected? That's right, the Roman empire! Now, remember Alexander? Remember how he was able to spread the Greek language throughout the known world? The Greek language was in place as the language of commerce and of foreign travelers from the earlier Greek empire of Alexander, and during the early part of the Roman empire, Roman rule provided safe travel. The followers of Jesus, because of the common language previ-ously established and of the good roads currently available, could quickly spread the gospel message of God's redemptive love and salvation. Yes, yes, yes... it DOES matter!! Not only that, but the book of Daniel records hundreds of years before the fact a prophetic understanding of the exact flow of history from the Babylonians to the Persians to the Greeks to the Romans, and then the coming of Messiah!! Evidently, the flow of history is important enough to God to convey it through the Bible, so let's let His standard be our own. History does have a flow, a big picture, an understandable message. And learning history is so much more memorable and meaningful when we see the overall view.

If you are at this point wringing your hands and saying, "Overview, overview, who can teach ME an overview?", help is on the way. A four-hour audiocassette entitled *What in the World's Going On Here—A Judeo-Christian Primer of World History* by me is available to give you a quick overview from the perspective that God has been sovereignly and intimately involved in human history from the first moment of creation. This is a hold-on-to-your-hat whirlwind tour of history that I put together to help parents make sense of stuff they never learned—or have forgotten they learned—in school.

For high school students, Cornerstone Curriculum Project has just released a new program, *Worldviews of the Western World*. It is a three-year program covering such subjects as literature (ancient, medieval, and modern), politics, economics, art history, music history, humanities, science history, philosophy and theology. The first year compares the Greco-Roman worldview with the Christian worldview; the second year compares the Renaissance with the Reformation; the third year compares the Judeo-Christian worldview with Modernism. The thorough grounding and deep understanding given in this extensive course is well worth the time invested.

The third and final point is to tell the story. History is best learned in story form. After all, even God Himself uses stories to teach us biblical truths in history. The biographies of Abraham, Moses, Joshua, David, Daniel, Esther, Mary, Jesus, Peter, Paul, and others tell the stories of the people through whose lives we learn about God's ways. What a wonderfully interesting means by which God has chosen to teach us. He used people *in history* to convey lessons for today.

Other stories one can read—about the Pilgrims, George Washington, Hudson Taylor, astronaut James Irwin, Corrie ten Boom, and others—will convey to the reader the sense of being there in historical time periods. It's *so* easy to remember names, dates, and places when you've "been there." Biographies, autobiographies, historical fiction, classics, diaries, journals, and poetry (try "Paul Revere's Ride" by Longfellow to get a taste of that portentous night) are the best way of capturing the essence of history. From that platform of "being there," studying history can take off with our motto "The sky's the limit." Eat historic food, wear historic costumes, play historic games, build miniature Mayflower ships, study ancient maps, listen to historic music, frame masterpieces of art. Ask questions about why the people did what they did, what were the results of these choices, what would have happened had different choices been made. Discuss the history that you are making right now. What choices are you making that will affect other people's lives? Ask hypothetical questions: What would you have done if *you* had been at the signing of the Declaration of Independence? Would you have had the courage to remain at Plymouth Plantation after the disastrous first winter? What would you have said to Pharaoh (or to God) when the firstborn died throughout Egypt? Consider the importance of the individual and the freedom each individual has to make choices. How has this impacted human history? Has it brought about curses or blessings? When? How? Why? How can we, using this freedom to choose, impact history as a blessing ourselves?

Don't allow history to sit on the shelf, in the book, being a mere exercise in memorization. Eat it, act it, wear it, think about it!

The sky's the limit!

Q. *Science was the one subject in school that I avoided as much as possible. How are my children going to learn anything about science from me?*

A. Science is often the bugaboo for nonscientist homeschool parents. (I know this from personal experience.) Having the opportunity at conventions to meet many different scientists sympathetic to homeschooling, I invariably buttonholed as many of them as possible to ask, "What do we, the science ignoramuses, do about science?" Here are some of the invaluable responses I received:

✒ The first point, and probably the most foreign to us nonscientists, is let your students play in the dirt! Let them (accompanied by you) hike in the mountains, walk in the forests, play by the beach, explore the desert, climb rocks, observe birds, watch the clouds, listen to the thunder. In short, get them *out* into God's creation, the first and best place for them to begin learning about science. Your students will begin to learn about the systems God has designed for the natural world: erosion, gravity, ecosystems, symbiosis, forestry, geology, oceanography, ornithology, meteorology, and on and on and ology.

The good friend and scientist who told me this, Monte Swan, is a professional geologist. Monte introduces homeschooling students to the science of geology by taking them out to look at huge rock cuts in the earth. As the students observe and study these rocks, Monte translates to them the "language" of the rocks, the story they tell. The students come away with a solid introduction to geology. More important than that, they think geology is *fascinating!* (I might not have flunked geology lab in college if my teacher had used this exciting method.)

Although you may not have access to Monte's expertise in geology, you can still learn from his method. Expose your children to rocks out in the "wild," look at the rocks, talk about what you see, and bring a book describing geological formations that will translate their story for you. Again, as in the case of history, you can learn right alongside your children.

⟨⟩ The second bit of wisdom gleaned from buttonholed scientists is experiment, experiment, experiment! Children need to learn how wondrous God's laws of nature are by experimenting with such things as dry ice, vinegar and soda, straws, magnets, earthworms, and balloons. Admittedly, experimenting is not a bookish endeavor, nor is it usually tidy. But you can always clean up your kitchen, and the tremendous value in experimenting more than offsets the extra work involved.

A few years ago we were selling books at the Wyoming State Homeschool Convention. It was not very crowded at the convention, which is not surprising, since Wyoming has the least number of people per square mile in the nation. One of the featured speakers at this convention was Jane Hoffman, the Backyard Scientist. She is a wonderful, exciting, bubbly, and adventurous (she blows things up on stage) speaker who loves working with children. My son (and resident budding scientist) Michael attached himself to Jane for the whole convention. Jane allowed him to be her helper on stage with all of her wild science experiments. Michael also had Jane's permission to hang around her booth all weekend, experimenting with aluminum foil, batteries, wires, light bulbs, chemicals, dry ice, and more. Jane was absolutely delighted to allow Michael to experiment to his heart's content and was more than recompensed when Michael created a working flashlight from bits of this and that. Did *I* learn some lessons that weekend!! It is utterly and completely necessary to encourage your young scientists by giving them the "stuff" of experiments and letting them play with it.

There are many good books available about experimenting using household materials (a great place to start). We really enjoy the *Backyard Scientist* books, since Jane Hoffman makes things so easy to understand. There are also Janice Van Cleave's books: *Chemistry for Every Kid, Physics for Every Kid, Astronomy for Every Kid,* among others. If you look around, you can find books of experiments for many different areas of scientific discovery. The key is to *use them.*

⚬ Use science programs that really get children to interact with the material being taught. It is not enough to look at a picture in a science textbook and read a few paragraphs about a plant, an animal, the stars, electricity, the chemistry of the blood, etc. We need to offer materials that teach science from a hands-on, discovery-oriented, thought-provoking approach.

This is more involved than simply experimenting with your children. For their understanding to systematically develop, with a comprehension of increasingly complex scientific knowledge, it is important to use a systematic program. (I am assuming you are a nonscientist. If you are very capable in science, you will already understand how to teach step by step in a systematic way. More power to you!!!)

Alta Vista is a unit study program based on science. It contains a mammoth amount of information and is very carefully and thoughtfully arranged. Because the people writing the programs for *Alta Vista* are well trained in the four learning styles, these unit study books are written to appeal to all four learning styles. It is well worth the effort to track down a copy of *Alta Vista* and consider it for your family. The study books are available from Family Christian Academy in Nashville, Tennessee.

Another excellent science program is *Science: The Search* from Cornerstone Curriculum Project. Available in four levels covering grades K–8, this program actively engages your students in the scientific thought process. Observation, recording, experimentation, and discussion are all integral parts of this curriculum. I don't know about your children, but mine love to discuss what they are studying and learning. Therefore, I love how David Quine equips us with script to dialogue with our children about what they are discovering.

So, the main ingredients to an extraordinary science program are (1) get to know the outdoors—sun, wind, rain, rocks, dirt, plants, animals; (2) allow for messy, crazy experiments even if they end in failure (remember Edison and his light bulb); and (3) choose a systematic, discovery-oriented program to develop an overall understanding of science. The sky's the limit!

Q. *I can't carry a tune in a bucket, and the only musical thing I play is the radio. How do I give my children an adequate education in music when I never had one myself?*

A. Music is, I believe, one of God's most delightful gifts to us. It is worthy of the time and trouble, the thought and expense that are required. To give our children an appreciation and understanding of music and to equip them in whatever way possible to make music is a legacy they will enjoy for a lifetime. The beauty and enrichment the study of music will bring to your entire family will do far more than just impact your children's academics. It can change the entire atmosphere of your home.

As with art, the study of music can be divided into two main areas: becoming an appreciative audience for it and becoming a skilled creator of it. We thus need to expose our children (and ourselves) to music history/appreciation through the wonderful classics in music and learn how to create music, whether through singing or playing an instrument (or both). I realize that this is easier said than done (especially for the non-musician), but many splendid resources are available.

To become familiar with the masterpieces in music, you will need either a tape player or a CD player (we still have a stereo phonograph with hundreds of classical records, but new records have become impossible to find and are basically obsolete). A CD player is by far the best choice (if you have that luxum) since its sound is the closest thing to actually being there.

Several books will help you get started on your musical odyssey. Patrick Kavanaugh's *A Taste for the Classics* describes the different types of classical music, from orchestral, choral, opera, and concerto to chamber music. The author also includes his recommended list of "your first thousand pieces" to listen to! Included with the book is a marvelous CD with several classical selections, just to give you a taste.

Mr. Kavanaugh, a thoroughly knowledgeable conductor and musician, has also written *The Spiritual Lives of the Great Composers*. This fascinating book looks at such composers as Handel, Bach, Haydn, Mozart, Beethoven, Wagner, and Dvorak. Not all of these composers were writing from a Christian worldview, but Mr. Kavanaugh has done an admirable job of compiling quotes, excerpts from letters, etc. that illustrate each composer's understanding of God.

My most-often-used book of composers is *The Gift of Music* by Jane Stuart Smith and Betty Carlson. Arranged chronologically from the late 1500s to the mid-1900s, this wonderful resource gives a brief bio, a description of the music, a recommended listening list, and the overriding worldview of thirty-six composers. With all of our university-level work in music, we never learned about the worldview of the composers. We consider this book an absolute must for your music history studies.

Edith Schaeffer's *Forever Music*, is a book worth reading. In her own inimitable style, Mrs. Schaeffer weaves together the stories of the building of a Steinway baby grand piano and the building of her own marriage to Dr. Francis Schaeffer. Within this amazing story, we are taken backstage to discover how a master piano technician, Franz Mohr, tunes and cares for the Steinway concert grands available to performing artists worldwide. Beyond being a wonderful, miraculous story in its own right, this book explores the importance of music to people, the importance of music to God, and the eternal nature of music in worship.

To build a quality musical library of classics can be an expensive (but worthwhile) proposition. We have recently joined one of those "order so many CDs/tapes for only a small amount..." and then receive their mailings every month. The recordings are *fabulous*, and when they have a sale, the prices are unbeatable. If you are interested in learning more, write BMG Classical Music Service, PO Box 91415, Indianapolis, IN 46291-0036. (Tell them you read about it here.)

A marvelous hook for classical music for children is *The Classical Kid's Collection*, a collection of five different tapes/CDs: "Beethoven Lives Upstairs," "Mozart's Magic Fantasy," "Mr. Bach Comes To Call," "Vivaldi's Ring of Mystery," and "Tchaikovsky Discovers America." In our own family, this series of intriguing stories surrounding a classical composer was the means of grabbing our children's interest in classical music. Before listening to these tapes, our children would grit their teeth when we played recordings of this type of music. "Please Mom, can't we listen to something else?" But after hearing the stories of these composers come to life, the children were eager and enthusiastic to listen to this marvelous music. And their appreciation for classical music has continued to grow.

An excellent music history/appreciation program, complete with tapes or CDs, is Cornerstone Curriculum's *Music and Moments with the*

Masters. This four-year program includes the book *The Gift of Music* (previously described) and numerous wonderful recordings. After completing the four-year program, a student (and family) may go on to study *Classical Composers and the Christian WorldView,* which includes six recordings and a seventy-five-page study guide.

The main ingredient for music history/appreciation is to begin listening. The complementary ingredient is to begin reading about what you are listening to, who composed it, and why. If you are very familiar with one area of music, stretch into another area. We have recently begun a study of opera (!) and are having a marvelous time listening to "Figaro, Figaro, Figaro, Figaro...." Though much of this style of music is foreign to our ears, listening to and reading about it is helping to make it our own. So, whether you are a novice or a veteran, stretch yourself and LISTEN!

Teaching someone to play a musical instrument when you do not know how to play is nearly impossible. Then, as homeschooling parents, what is possible? What *can* we do at home, and what are our away-from-home options?

At home, you can sing. Family singalongs are wonderful, fun, and free entertainment. Hymns, choruses, folk songs, nursery rhymes, and Christmas carols are easily sung. Invest in a hymnal, a children's songbook, a treasury of folk songs, and other collections of simple-to-sing songs. Any of your family members with an ear for it can add harmony to your melody line ("Mama sang bass, Daddy sang tenor..."). Try your skill at singing rounds like "Row, Row, Row Your Boat" or "Three Blind Mice." This builds a good ear for hearing harmonies and is a wonderful skill that can develop through the years. (My dear friend in college, Mary Beth, and I used to practice singing simple songs one-half step apart. It sounded terrible but was a tremendous aid in developing our musical skill.)

If singing a cappella (without accompaniment) seems too intimidating, put on a recording of worship songs, folk songs, or children's songs, and sing along. Integrity Music has produced a huge number of worship tapes for both adults and children. The tapes are very easy to sing along with and offer the added benefit of learning new songs with which to praise God. Hear & Learn Publications (the company I formed with three other musicians) has produced several American folk song tapes and books. We have heard from numerous families that their children love to sing along with our tapes—and they learn American history in the process. "Wee Sing" is another producer of a number of tapes for children's singalongs. There are many different recordings of children's music—some traditional, some specifically Christian, some worth having, others not. You will have to find what works for your family, but don't neglect the benefit of singing along with these recordings.

Before leaving the family singalong, let me encourage you to dust off that old guitar, ukelele, banjo, washtub bass, tambourine, conga drum, trumpet, violin, clarinet, or piano. Even if what comes out is not "perfect," playing an instrument can still be fun! And your children may be encouraged to pick up one of these instruments and start learning it for themselves. Sometimes, just having an instrument available may be the spark required to set your children ablaze.

When I was about twelve, my grandfather gave me his old guitar (for those who know about these things, it was a Martin F-hole). I messed around with it for a few years, but the summer I turned fifteen, I purchased a "Learn the Guitar" book and taught myself to play. Granted, I would be a far better guitar player if I had received lessons. Still, it was enough instruction for me to be able to play and accompany my folk singing in concerts, play around campfires for Christian gatherings, lead worship in churches and small groups, etc. I also learned to play banjo (after I was married) by this same self-study method. Though I don't play for anyone besides my family, the banjo has added a tremendously fun aspect to our family music making.

Melody has taught herself to play recorder, using some Usborne books and my recorder. We had the opportunity to observe a professional recorder player at a concert and asked her advice about learning to play. She suggested becoming familiar with more than one size recorder, so Melody asked Grandma for an alto recorder for Christmas. She often asks me to play duets with her, which adds another dynamic to our family music making. It *is* possible to learn enough from a book to be able to enjoy yourself.

Beyond our own family singalongs and learning to play an instrument with a book, what can we offer our children?

⚬ Is there a choir at your church that your family could participate in? You will learn a lot about music in that kind of setting.

⚬ Do you have or can you rent a piano? Are your children interested in learning to play it? Can you afford piano lessons? Even if it is for a short time, piano lessons are another gift that will bless your child for a lifetime.

⁓ What about other instruments? Is there a homeschool band in your area or a Christian school band you can access? What about joining the band in the local public school? (That has never been an option we wished to pursue, but I know of others who have been quite happy with the result. It is certainly something to pray about.)

⁓ Do you have a family member or a church member who is skilled in playing an instrument and would be willing to offer lessons?

⁓ Talk to your local music (instrument) store. It may offer reasonably priced lessons on the instrument your child wishes to pursue. If not, it probably knows where to look.

When I was in junior high, I decided to play the oboe. If you've never had the opportunity to hear a beginner play one, suffice it to say that the sound is something like a dying cow. My parents evidently didn't feel that I was progressing fast enough (or their ear drums had had enough!), so they found a local college student who was willing to give me private lessons "for a song." It was a wonderful experience for me, and my parents were soon able to better appreciate the sounds emanating from my bedroom.

The study of music is something you can enjoy and by which you will be enriched for the rest of your life. Listen to the best, read to understand, and create the music you most delight in—whether instrumental or vocal, classical or jazz, American or African, lively or stately, longhair or popular. Remember, the sky's the limit!

Recommended Reading

You CAN Teach Your Child Successfully (Grades 4–8) by Ruth Beechick
    Mrs. Beechick has some fabulous ideas about teaching your children. Her perspective on home education is very encouraging, and the suggestions and models she gives can make a tremendous difference in how we do what we do.

The Enjoyment of Music by Machlis, published by W.W. Norton
    High school/college program with text and recordings, this is one of the most excellent collections available. It includes beautiful artwork in the text and recordings from the earliest printed music through the most modern.

Benjamin West and His Cat, Grimalkin by Marguerite Henry
One of my all-time favorite stories! This is about the father of American painting, Benjamin West, and the unorthodox way he began to paint—with brushes made from the hairs of his cat!

Chapter 10

~∞∞∞~

Evaluations:
Testing Your Progress

*O*nce a week I made my way to Sister Consuelo's office. A German nun, Sister Consuelo held a master's degree in French and traveled to France as often as possible. She had been recommended as an exceptional French teacher and was willing to tutor me privately. Early in our relationship, having never experienced one-on-one teaching, I blithely entered her office unprepared.

I had no place to hide. Not knowing my lesson, I discovered that no one else was around to distract the teacher. Sister Consuelo asked me this, she asked me that, and silence was my only answer. An excellent and impressive communicator, she made me painfully aware that a student must learn the material each week or else the time together is wasted.

Since I had breezed through school, receiving A's almost effortlessly, this was indeed a rude awakening, but one I became most grateful for. The lessons Sister Consuelo imparted were far greater than merely the French language. This dedicated teacher taught me to study, to be thoroughly prepared, to be diligent in what I undertook. And she eloquently demonstrated to me that a student cannot hide his or her ignorance when examined in a tutorial setting.

Our Journal

When we moved to South Dakota from Washington, we received a shock. The law in South Dakota required each school site (including homeschools) to be inspected by a representative of the local school district. We were quite concerned that our alternative means of instruction was a little too alternative for the tastes of a school district, though it was obvious that our children were getting a thorough education.

Bill visited with the principal, the designated representative, to discuss with him exactly what we should expect during the inspection. The principal's comments caused both a little encouragement and a little apprehension. We were encouraged because the local school was experimenting with a multi-disciplinary approach in a few subjects, so the principal was familiar with using a non-traditional approach to education. We were also apprehensive because we didn't know just how far on the non-traditional scale he would be willing to allow us to go. It's one thing to combine a few subjects, it's quite another to throw out the textbooks!

Our inspection was not scheduled until winter, so I was able to put it out of my mind for a few months. The children and I had grand times of studying autumn leaves, building bird houses, reading classics, floating iron weights, learning geography through songs and games, discovering world history from the perspective that God is sovereign, memorizing poetry, writing mysteries, and more. But as the day approached, I felt impending doom close in on me.[1]

The day before the principal was to visit us, I felt God encourage me to treat this visit as a show-and-tell—an opportunity to openly share the abundance and delight of our homeschool with a public school official. Rather than view him as the enemy, we made this man a welcome visitor.

Knowing that part of the visit was to examine the materials we were using in our school, I had gathered up armfuls of books and set them in piles by subject. We had stacks three and four feet high of science, readers, history, literature, music history, art, foreign language, geography, and more. Several educational games, our computer, musical instruments, and math manipulatives sat out in plain view. Samples of our

---

1. Had the inspection not been required by law, we would not have permitted the state to examine our homeschool.

children's stories, artwork, birdhouses, math papers, and science projects were on display around the room. And the children were ready.

The moment the principal entered the house, we were filled with joy to be able to share our homeschool. The children eagerly showed him their handiwork, explaining their favorite subjects. When the principal asked for the titles of our textbooks (to fill in the necessary questionnaire), I pointed to the stacks of books. He gulped slightly and said, "I have only a few lines to write down your book titles...uh, do you have *any* textbooks?" I am sure he was relieved when I pulled out a few math, language arts, and history textbooks. The next difficult moment came when he asked about our hours of operation. I answered, truthfully, that we are basically in school from the moment we get up until we go to sleep, since we are learning all of the time by constantly reading books, sharing what we've learned, discussing history, etc. He was stymied by that one but finally asked if it would be all right if he wrote down that we maintained regular school hours. I was quite content with that, so he was able to successfully complete the next section of his questionnaire. Finally, he asked if we had any supplementary educational materials such as a computer or educational games. The children joyfully showed him all of our "stuff," including historic games, Geo-Safari, music tapes, foreign language tapes, and the computer. The principal put a checkmark by the question, folded his paper, and tried to make his way out of our house. But the children, not to be deterred, kept displaying this project and that, wanting to read their stories, showing him their latest cartoons, until I finally corralled them, allowing the poor, overwhelmed man to make good his escape.

We have no idea what impact our school had on this man, but we had been blessed with the joy of the Lord and delighted in sharing the good things of our homeschool. We felt that our school had passed the test with flying colors in the sight of the law. Though I have never had such an experience either before or since, it was good for us to be able to articulate all of the things our children study, what they are learning, how our school is structured, and what our goals are. God, in this experience, truly turned our "mourning into dancing" (Psalm 30:11).

How am I going to know whether my kids are learning?

This is one question asked constantly by new homeschoolers.

Having been schooled in a classroom setting with thirty other students, we initially have no conception of the dynamics of a tutorial educational style. As you continue to teach your children, you become increasingly confident in what your children know, what they struggle with, and what they are not yet ready to learn.

Having said that, let me offer some suggestions of ways you can informally test your children, of ways your children can display what they have learned. The following are ideas that many homeschoolers utilize in evaluating their children's progress:

ᕫ Observation/examination. Look over their shoulders as they work. Listen to the things they share with their siblings or with you. "This is a *great* book! It lists all these weird but true facts about the Civil War." That remark tells me that my child is (a) reading, (b) comprehending, and (c) retaining information, along with (d) the content of his studies and (e) the focus of his interests. What are *your* children saying?

Take a lesson from birdwatchers: carefully observe your children at work. It will become evident in what subjects they are thriving and in what areas they need more support and more practice.

ᕫ Discussion. Talk with your children about what they are learning or about what *you* are learning. Ask questions, listen to their answers. Give thoughtful answers to *their* questions. You will be amazed when you really listen to your children's thoughts.

Remember that discussions will flow in a caring, responsive environment; they will not flow in an inquisition atmosphere. We need to examine the settings in which we ourselves feel most at home sharing our thoughts and then try to sensitively create that kind of environment for our children. For instance, I love the conversational atmosphere of candlelight, classical music, and a roaring fire in the woodstove. My children respond warmly to this congenial setting when given the opportunity to share their thoughts, though they also enjoy a cafe booth with French fries, or the top of a grassy knoll under shade trees.

ᕫ Narration. Discussed more fully in the book *For the Children's Sake* by Susan Schaeffer Macaulay, narration simply means allowing your children to tell in their own words what a story was about. The children narrate back to you (not parrot, mind you) what they have learned or what you just read out loud or what they read to themselves. It is very enlightening to listen to your children narrate—they often get more from the story than you think. In fact, they may have picked up on some nuance that you would not have expected.

Be open to what your children consider important. Remember Valerie Bendt's son who thought the best part of the story about Patrick Henry was the fact that he did not have to wear shoes until he was nine years old. We need to allow our children their designated important events to stand, even if later we want to enlarge their understanding of what else was important in a story, biography, etc. Obviously, if our children have not listened and cannot accurately narrate what was in a story, the story needs to be reread with a little more enthusiasm. We need to be careful not to stomp on a newly budding creative thinker.

⚭ Projects/presentations. Rather than have your students answer true/false questions, guess on multiple choice, or fill in blanks, you could utilize a project/presentation that offers a creative, expressive way for students to demonstrate what they have learned.

Projects can range from very simple science experiments conducted for the family to elaborate posters on 4x8 sheets of plywood diagramming the cause/effect relationship of people and events during a historical time period. They could include artwork, crafts, experiments, table displays, charts and diagrams, architectural designs, and more.

Presentations could include describing a project before an audience—"You just add water to this dry ice and...voilà! An erupting volcano before your very eyes!!"—or presenting a skit, puppet show, dramatic recitation, Shakespearean play, debate, etc., any of which could demonstrate what has been learned.

Several years ago, we initiated our Homeschool Presentation Night (as described in Chapter Eight) to give our children a chance to have an audience. We have invited friends, family, and other homeschooling families to attend, though often the audience is composed of just the five of us. One of the best results of our presentation night is that it causes our children to learn the materials thoroughly. [Diana's maxim: The one who has to teach others is the one who learns a subject best!] Our children will go to great lengths to prepare a good presentation for this night, and we've seen marvelous creativity unleashed in each of them as they have had this opportunity. It's also been rip-roaring family fun, as they have performed puppet shows, sung a cappella, recited hysterically funny poetry, drawn cartoon portrayals of economic principals, and more. It has certainly been worth all the time and trouble to prepare for these nights, and these presentations are a far greater evaluation of what our students have actually learned than a test would show. We highly recommend this method to you.

⊸ Tailor-made lessons. Ask your children what *they* are interested in learning. It is much easier to learn what you want to know than to learn what you have no interest in knowing. Isn't it thus obvious that your children will learn readily and enthusiastically if they have some say in the matter about what they are to learn? This is not to say that you cease teaching grammar or math or phonics or spelling (often the "groaners" of education), but it does mean you could try to balance out the "groaners" with the "grinners."

We make it a point every year to sit down with our children and ask each of them, "What would you like to learn about this year?" The subjects suggested have been as varied as horticulture and World War II airplanes, but we try to find ways to incorporate at least some of their interests into the planning of our school for the year. The creative, unusual suggestions offered by our children have stretched us, caused us to learn things we would never have thought about learning, and wonderfully benefited us all.

The preceding have all been relationship-based evaluators used to discover what our children are learning. There are also formal evaluations, which we are probably more familiar with, that we can utilize.

Learning to take tests is a skill that will benefit our children throughout their lives, so we have made it a point to teach our children how to take tests. "Read the questions very carefully." "Answer first the questions you know, then go back to consider the questions you didn't get easily." "Check your work." "If it is multiple choice and you do not find the answer listed that you expect, reread the question and make sure you understand what is being asked."

If you yourself were not a good test taker, make it a point to learn the concepts along with your children. You can get books devoted to teaching your children how to take tests from your local library.

Though we prefer the informal, relational approach and seldom give our children tests in their regular course of study, you may choose to test your children on a more regular basis. There are tests listed in textbooks, questions at the end of a chapter (both in textbooks and sometimes in educational living books), tests you can create based on what your children have been learning, and the once-a-year standardized tests (discussed in more detail later in this chapter).

One important concept to remember is this: Tests evaluate how well you have been teaching or how well the materials have done their job more than how "good" the student is. Don't berate a student for not knowing something. Use the student's lack of knowledge in a particular area as a sign for you to go back and reteach an area, perhaps using different materials.

Another means of formal evaluation is professional assessment. We know of many professionally trained educators who are quite sympathetic with homeschoolers (some of them are homeschoolers themselves). Such people can sit down with your students and evaluate how they are doing in school—whether they are at grade level, comprehend the materials being taught, and have acquired the necessary skills to advance to the next level. Professional evaluations are a wonderful alternative to standardized testing (if you have a choice), since they are nonthreatening and friendly and the evaluator can learn a lot without the child's ever realizing he or she is being tested. If you desire to have your child evaluated by a professional, ask your local support group for its recommendations, and be aware that it will probably cost you a professional's fee.

How am I going to know whether these are the right books?

Do you remember my story under "Our Journal" in Chapter One about buying an expensive set of curriculum materials, using it for thirty days, and then realizing that they were the **wrong books**? Unfortunately, that is *not* an uncommon happening among homeschool families. To serve the needs of our children, we need to consider how to regularly evaluate the materials we are using, regardless of how much they cost or of who else uses them.

Let us begin with the word *curriculum*. The dictionary defines curriculum as a course of study, but to look at the root word from which we derive *curriculum*, we'll find that the original root word means "to run." To run? Does that describe your current curriculum materials? Do your students run with what they are learning? Or are they, instead, being dragged along, kicking and screaming, with their feet plowing two narrow grooves behind them?

Picture, if you will, what "running" with your educational materials would look like. Your students would be enthusiastic in their studies, full of new thoughts and questions, eager to continue learning, and desirous of sharing with others what is being learned. Is that a picture of your learners? If not, are you willing to consider making some changes?

The opposing picture is much more common to education, especially public schools and private schools, but it is even found among homeschoolers. The student is being dragged by the curriculum "master" through the "Slough of Who Cares," uninterested, uninvolved, and unwilling to continue. The only reason the child makes his or her way through the course of study is that there is no choice, no freedom involved. Is this a picture of your learners? If it is, are you willing to break out of the mold and make some changes?

Ask yourself and your children, "Are the books we've chosen doing what we want them to do? Are they provoking discussions? Are they stimulating more questions? Are the children showing enthusiasm for what they are learning? Are they interested in continuing to learn about this area?" [Diana's maxim: You can lead a child to knowledge, but you can't make him drink. So sweeten the waters!!]

If your children are responding negatively to the materials you are using, here are a couple of points to consider:

⁓ Is the book extremely challenging? Perhaps you need to help your children gear up for this book, as it may seem overwhelming to them. The first time I asked Isaac to read *Robinson Crusoe*, he balked. Just trying to read the first paragraph left him speechless. So we discussed the book, the style of writing, the author's intentions in writing the book, etc., until Isaac felt he understood enough to begin reading. It was not *easy*, but he soon began to enjoy the book thoroughly.

We have seen this many times with our children. If a book looks hard, the child is not interested—until we begin to unfold the mysteries contained within. Overcoming and surmounting such challenges have made our children better students *and* have made them more willing to tackle even greater challenges. Don't necessarily allow your students to back away from a challenge (if it is within their ability to accomplish it), but DO help them get started, DO encourage them along the way, and DO listen carefully to their complaints. Perhaps the task *is* too hard for their skills at this point.

⁓ On the other hand, is the book receiving constant criticism? If your children make a constant stream of comments concerning specific problems—"It uses little kid sentences." "We read the same stuff last week." "It hurts my eyes." "I can't read it." "It's too technical." "The illustrations are ugly." "This book is *not* interesting."—you need to make a decision. At this point, you can say to your children:

"I chose this book for a specific reason. (Name the reason.) I know it is not the most wonderful book you have ever read, but I think you will learn something important from this book. Would you like to work on it together?" (Find a way to make it as interesting as possible.)

OR

"Hmmm. You are right. Let me go through this book and choose only the sections that I thought were important for you to study. Will that help?" (Editing is a homeschool mom's birthright!)

OR

"You are absolutely right! The saying You can't tell a book by its cover has proven true this time! What say we put it in the basket of books to sell at the next used book sale?" (Then you all dance merrily around the room!)

This is an important but often misunderstood point. As the home-school parent, YOU ARE IN CHARGE! Not the textbook, not the living book, not the scope and sequence, not a program, not your neighbor. YOU! So, if a book doesn't work, YOU can make the decision to get rid of it. Only you are in the position to see whether a certain book or program is causing your children to run. If it isn't, you have the freedom and the responsibility to find something that will.

A subject can be studied from several different perspectives. Even among traditional textbook providers, there are many different approaches. If you have trouble with one kind, try another. If, after doing some investigating of your children's learning styles, you see that your students require a completely different type of approach, take a deep breath and try it.

If you have never experienced it, it's hard to comprehend the absolute joy in your homeschool of studying things the students are interested in, using books they think are fascinating. It is such a contrast to the drudgery we so often face. A picture comes to mind of an historic tall ship, complete with masts and sails. When there was no wind to fill the sails, when there was no current to move the ship along, when they were becalmed, sometimes the sailors would have to get into the long boats and, using oars, row with all of their might to move the sailing ship a short way. It was incredibly labor intensive, exhausting, debilitating, and fairly ineffectual. But when the wind came up, the sails would fill and the ship would glide, under the helmsman's touch, nearly effortlessly through the waters. Our children's studies can be the same way, and "finding the wind" is not difficult if you are using curriculums, books, and materials that your children find exciting.

How am I going to know whether my teaching is successful?

Most homeschool moms start the first day of class feeling that they are not quite prepared. Don't let that paralyze you. It will become easier to prepare as you get more experience, and your lesson plans will be better as you develop confidence. What is most important to keep in mind is this: You will do just fine as long as your care for your kids motivates you (which is why you are homeschooling in the first place, right?).

Your function is really that of a facilitator, one who provides the opportunities that make schoolwork easier and more accessible. You are there to facilitate your children's growth in learning. Set before them a bountiful table of knowledge and allow them to feast to their heart's content. Believe me, they will learn.

Consider the responsibilities of a farmer. He must prepare the soil (to cultivate a hunger for receiving the seeds), place the seeds in the soil, water the seeds buried in the soil, and restrict the growth of weeds. The seed, however, does most of the work as God enables it. The seed pushes through the soil, sending roots down deep. It grows up, flowers, and produces more seeds. You are just like that farmer. You do have responsibilities to cultivate the good soil in your children's hearts and minds. You need to plant good seed, keep it watered, and restrict the growth of weeds (television comes immediately to mind), but your children will do most of the work of learning, growing, and becoming fruitful in their knowledge. After you have planted, weeded, and watered, relax!

It is also important for you to continue to be a student yourself. You need to be reading good books—whether on homeschooling, cross-country skiing, embroidery, learning styles, ethnic cooking, or whatever seems interesting—to further your own growth. The very best teachers are enthusiastic students! Allow yourself a bit of time to be a student.

Have you ever heard someone say, "If you don't have a goal, you are sure to miss it!?" It is true, and it is critical to consider in our home-schools. We need to set goals for our children's growth and periodically check in to see whether we are accomplishing what was planned. For instance, one year Bill and I were very aware that Michael needed to have some concentrated instruction in spelling. We listed that subject in our goals for the year and made it an everyday priority. After three months, Michael's placement (determined through testing) had moved up three grades. If we had not made this a priority goal, I would not have spent that kind of intensive time on this subject, and Michael would probably still be floundering in spelling.

If you need some outside help in setting goals, look through some scope and sequence materials to see what children are supposed to be learning at each grade level (though please don't be bound hand and foot by someone else's opinion of what should be learned when).

If your children take standardized tests each year, use them as possible indicators of priority goals for the following year. When your children take a standardized test, though it does NOT show you how intelligent, bright, loving, creative, or wise they are, it CAN show you what areas you need to strengthen in their education. For example, one year we discovered that Melody had some difficulties in her math computation. Her understanding of the math concepts was excellent, but her speed in computation was dismal. The next year we listed "develop speed in math skills" as a goal for her. Melody spent time every day working with the basic math facts and little by little developed the necessary speed. Remember, standardized tests reflect more what the teacher needs to strengthen in her teaching than how the student is doing. Use them merely as a tool to help you determine your children's goals.

If your children are not meeting their goals, you need to find out why. Are the goals realistic? (Make sure you do not list that your six-year-old needs to conquer calculus this year.) Are your materials effective and interesting? Do you need to change your presentation? (Read *The Seven Laws of the Learner* by Dr. Bruce Wilkinson.) Are you working with the learning styles of your children? Is your teaching style working with your children? Remember, you are there to serve the needs of your students, not the other way around. Are you connected to a support group? Such a group may be able to help you with teaching strategies. (This is certainly a case of the biblical concept of "the older women teaching the younger." Take advantage of it if you can.) Finally, and most importantly, pray and ask the Lord to give you His wisdom concerning your children's education. He who created each one unique can certainly give us understanding in how to effectively communicate with our own specific, individual children.

Charting Your Course

Lesson plans? Recordkeeping? What's a mother to do?

Since this is not my cup of tea, I asked Bill, the professional educator, to share with us some of the lessons he learned about lesson planning during his tenure as a schoolteacher. (Bill has taken over the lesson planning and recordkeeping for our school, and homeschooling has been on an even keel ever since.) Bill said that lesson planning can be pursued in a variety of ways, from sketchy to elaborate. Here are some examples.

◦∽◦ Just list topics:
Algebra—quadratic
Lit.—behavior
Science—chemicals
　　　This method is good when the lessons flow in a sequential nature and every day you do the subsequent lesson. If the teacher is very familiar with the materials, this is adequate.

◦∽◦ Note the page numbers of what is to be covered:
Algebra—pp. 237–239
Literature—pp. 7–26 *Captains Courageous*
Science—p. 106 *Marvels and Mysteries of Nature*
　　　This method is good for the concept minded—one who does not have to notate every little detail.

◦∽◦ Highlight the key points:
Algebra—quadratic formula
Literature—Why is Harvey so hard to get along with?
Science—nature's chemical warfare
　　　This is just to keep in mind an overview of what will be covered each day.

◦∽◦ Chart out an outline:
I. Algebra
　　　A. Page 237—Quadratic formula explain.
　　　B. Page 238—Quadratic formula practice.
　　　C. Page 239—Quadratic formula assign 1–10.
II. Literature—*Captains Courageous*, Rudyard Kipling
　　　A. Pages 7–12　Harvey's behavior on the ship
　　　B. Pages 12–18　Harvey's behavior below decks
　　　C. Pages 19–26　Harvey's behavior with Capt. Troop
III. Science—*Mysteries and Marvels of Nature*, Usborne
　　　A. Page 106　bombardier beetle
　　　B. Page 106　lubber grasshopper

C. Page 106 sand wasp

You don't need to be a master of the outline form, just write down the flow of the day's lessons.

ᔆ Write out each detail:

Algebra: Page 237 Write example on whiteboard, discuss examples, then show proof for quadratic formula. Page 238 Do two samples together on whiteboard, Bobby solve three samples on whiteboard, check for understanding. Page 239 Assign numbers 1–10 in notebook. Due today.

Literature: Read together Chapter One of *Captains Courageous* by Rudyard Kipling. Determine why Harvey's behavior caused the others to not like him. Pages 7–12: Discuss how he spoke to the crew and passengers on the packet. Pages 12–18: Discuss how he spoke to Manny and Dan. Pages 19–26: Describe his conversation with Captain Troop. Then ask what were the other characters responses to Harvey. Finish by lunchtime.

Science: Page 106 in *Mysteries and Marvels of Nature* by Usborne. Discuss topic: God has built defense mechanisms into some insects that utilize chemical solutions. Painful spray—bombardier beetle: chemicals mixed in abdomen; sprayed at attacker at 1,000 pulses per second; vapor at approximately 100 degrees Celsius. Poison sting—painful jabs: sand wasp injects nerve poison in prey; 50 different chemicals identified in various species; results in itching to death. Nasty smell—lubber grasshopper: oozes foul-smelling froth; mixes air with phenol and quinones. 1:00–2:00.

Do this in pencil because it will become your journal. At the end of the day, simply erase whatever did not happen and include whatever extra things occurred.

Any of these plans can become a springboard for successive planning as well as a record of achievement.[2]

Record keeping can be as varied as lesson planning, depending on your state laws, your family needs, the coursework, ages of your students, and your style. It can be very detailed or very brief, kept in diary form or on the computer. It can be simply your lesson plans altered to reflect what actually occurred, kept hourly, daily, or weekly.

---

2. My style of lesson planning is jotting down topics, while Bill's is a combination of the more complex plans. Use whatever works best for you.

If your children do projects or presentations, keep a record of what they did (homemade books, artwork, tape recording, written reports, video recording, etc.), which will result in a portfolio of your students' accomplishments.

If you use a daily "To Do" list, have your children mark off each subject as they complete it and then compile the lists in a folder. This is a nearly painless form of record keeping, since the children are the "recorders," you don't have to remember what was accomplished, and it is finished at the end of each day.

A diary of lesson planning and record keeping would show the subjects covered during the day or week. Mark the date when each goal was accomplished and any accompanying remarks that would be pertinent. "Finished *Bridge Over the River Kwai*—will not recommend that to the next student!"

The most exhaustive record keeping would track the daily activities of each student, listing the accomplishments and the scores (grade). This daily score culminates in a final grade for the course. Schoolteachers use this method of record keeping, but it seems too heavy-handed for most homeschooling needs. However, if this seems like the best procedure for you and does not produce unnecessary stress in your children, go for it!

You can purchase preprinted record-keeping books, lesson planners, and schedulers from local teacher supply stores, from some homeschool mail order providers, or sometimes from a business/stationary supply store. You can also make your own forms using three-ring binders, spiral-bound notebooks, diaries, or computer-generated forms designed for your specific needs. The main idea is to get *something* and begin using it to help you set your goals and to evaluate how well the goals are being met. [Diana's maxim: The better the preparation, the easier the implementation.]

Part Three

❦

The Abundance

Chapter 11

❦

Serve the Lord with Gladness!
Family Ministry

*T*he homeschool convention in Casper, Wyoming, had come to an end. All the attendees, having gathered up their notes, curriculum purchases, and children, were long gone. Nearly all the vendors had packed up their wares and carted them out to vehicles waiting to travel to the next show. Only a few of the convention organizers were left in the building as my children and I carried out box after box of books from our exhibit table.

One of the highlights of this convention had been the "Teen Track" seminar by Joshua Harris, son of nationally known homeschool speaker Gregg Harris. Isaac, especially, had been blessed by Josh's humor, his heart, and his ministry to young people. All through the exhibit hall, people had been speaking of how wonderful Josh's talks were and how grateful they were for his willingness to come to their convention.

These comments were running through my mind as we carried out the seemingly endless supply of books when, passing by an open door, I saw something that made me stand stock still. Josh Harris, with not another soul in sight, was carefully vacuuming the nursery. I am absolutely certain that his contract with the convention organizers did *not* include vacuuming! But having seen a need, regardless of how "lowly" it was, Josh responded as a servant. No one else was there to see the servant's heart being displayed, but God knew. And so did I.

My pastor's wife would often tell her young sons, "A man of integrity does what is right, even when no one is watching." That day, Josh displayed the characteristics of a man of integrity. What joy was in my heart as I realized that this godly young man was a model for my own sons. May God give us the wisdom and grace to be men and women of integrity, and may He help us to raise our children to follow in His footsteps.

Our Journal

We have always done the normal things Christian parents do: gone to church with our children, prayed with them at night, read Bible stories, and talked with them about God. But as the Lord began to stretch us and deepen our relationship with Him, He showed us that it was important to include our children in other aspect of life. Over the past few years, our children have started spending time praying earnestly with us about direction: where to live, where to attend church, how to develop new friendships, ministry opportunities, business decisions, finances, and more.

Seeing a need to teach how to study the Bible, Bill began using the *Children's Inductive Bible Study* program by Janice Southerland with our children on a daily basis. It was an eye-opening experience to see the children delving into the Scriptures with a hunger to know. *Strong's Concordance* became a familiar tool, and the *Greek Lexicon* was in hot demand around our living room. Fantastic conversations kept erupting over things being learned, over questions of what was meant by this phrase, over issues mentioned in that phrase, over what it means to be a Christian in the nineties. Our children learned how to handle God's Word for themselves with increasing skill, which immeasurably deepened their relationship with Him.

At about the same time, our tiny church began Saturday morning intercessory prayer for our church, our community, the nation, and the world. After attending one of the prayer meetings, we quickly realized that this was something our children would benefit from. When invited, they responded with great enthusiasm (even though it meant getting up early on Saturday morning). For the past year, they have continued to faithfully attend the prayer meeting, even though they are usually the only children present. In fact, on some Saturday mornings when I would much rather be a lazybones and stay in bed, my children show up dressed and ready to go!

One of the latest events in our shared family ministry concerned establishing a new city ordinance. A few businesses in our little community suddenly brought in nude dancing. Many Christians were up in arms over this, sending letters to our city council and to the editor and doing all of the other things that moral people do when their town is threatened with blatant immorality. Our church's Saturday morning prayer meeting was exclusively devoted for a time to pray about this blight on our town. Then, as a further response, some of us discussed having prayer walks through downtown. Prayer walks are kind of like putting feet to your prayers. They enable you to go to and pray specifically, quietly, and unobtrusively over a certain place. When this idea was brought up in the prayer meeting, our children couldn't wait to start. They saw themselves as integral members of our prayer walk team, which, indeed, they were. Shortly after the prayer walks were established, the city council voted for an ordinance that would disallow that kind of dancing, and one of the two businesses shut down for lack of funds. Though our children know that there were many things that contributed to this victory, they felt that we also had played a significant part through the prayer walks.

This was not an artificial solution, nor one we tried to capitalize on, but was, we felt, simply obedience to God. Our children gladly followed in that obedience. And they saw the results.

Bill and I are coming to realize that much of the discipleship process with our children means simply bringing them alongside, doing what we do, letting them see how we live out our Christianity, eliminating the artificial separation between "adults'" and "children's" ministry. Many, many, many homeschooled children, having been discipled and taught by adults, having been in constant companionship of adults and not of peers, have shown themselves eager and able to do tasks usually considered fit only for adults. Intercession, decision making, self-employment, ministry, volunteer opportunities are a few of these.

The result is that our children are learning, as we also learn, who God is and how to trust Him in real life, in big decisions as well as the small ones. They are experiencing right alongside us what it means to wait on God. They are coming to understand, along with us, that prayer "availeth much" (James 5:16) and that the Bible contains all they need "for life and godliness" (2 Peter 1:3).

By the grace of God, they are living experientially, though imperfectly, the words of Deuteronomy 6:7, "And you shall teach them diligently unto your children, and shall talk of them when you sit down in your house, and when you walk by the way, and when you lie down, and when you rise up."

To Whom All Praise Is Due

In the first ten chapters we have been looking at different aspects of homeschooling—educational goals, styles, approaches, and subjects, the how-to's. But if we are to really go to the heart, to really enter into the "good life" of homeschooling, if we are to truly experience the abundant life Jesus promised, we must consider the most important aspect of all— our walk with the Lord. To be a Christian homeschool, it is not enough to use Christian textbooks and add a course in the Bible. We must take time to nurture our relationship with God Himself.

You see, abundant homeschooling *begins* with an abundant Christian life. And an abundant Christian life *begins* with an abundant relationship with our Savior and Lord. And an abundant relationship with our Savior and Lord *begins* with spending abundant time with Him. And when you *begin* to spend abundant time with Jesus Christ, through His Word and through prayer, abundant worship, praise, and thanksgiving will *begin* to flow *abundantly* out of your hearts. All of His paths "drip with abundance!" (Psalm 65:11)

Psalm 107 states over and over again, "Oh, that men would *give thanks* to the Lord for His goodness, and for His wonderful works to the children of men!" We, as individuals and as a family, need to take the time to discuss and meditate on the goodness of God and on His awesome, wonderful deeds. As we consider His goodness and His wonderful works, we will truly "enter His gates with thanksgiving, enter His courts with praise, be thankful to Him, and bless His name" (Psalm 100:4).

We once heard an evangelist by the name of Terry Law ask, "How many of you keep a list of prayer requests?" Nearly everyone in the room raised a hand. Then he asked a most thought-provoking question: "How many of you have a list of God's blessings in your life?" Only a few hands went up. Ouch! The point struck painfully home: so often when we pray, we focus on what *we* need, what *we* want, what *we* think is wrong, what *we* want changed. In our eagerness to "take it to the Lord in prayer," we usually forget what God has already given us—His goodness, His faithfulness, His answers, His wisdom, His compassion, His patience, His love, His grace, His mercy.

As we focus on God and His goodness, our homes can become literal fountains of praise and thanksgiving, bubbling up fragrantly and continuously to God. And those who come to our homes may just get wet! Our families can experientially live out I Thessalonians 5:16–18: "Rejoice *always*, pray *without ceasing*, in *everything* give thanks; for this is the will of God in Christ Jesus for you." As I often tell my children, "Always means ALWAYS! Everything means EVERYTHING!!"

If you have been asking, "How do I know God's will for me?", here is one of your answers. Always rejoice, pray continually, and give thanks all of the time, in every situation—and teach your children to do the same. "Mo-o-o-o-mmmmmm, the dishwasher is gushing water all over the kitchen floor!"—"Thank You, Jesus, that You know what is going on. Thank You that You promised to never leave me or forsake me—since I know You are here, can You please help me find a plumber, NOW???!!!"[1]

For us to know just how marvelous and wonderful our God is, we need to spend time studying and considering His Word. Think about the impossibility of finite, sinful, weak, ignorant, helpless mortals ever being able to comprehend, understand, and know an infinite, perfect, all-powerful, all-knowing, limitless Being, unless He chose to make Himself known to them. What incredible joy to know that He *did* choose to reveal Himself! We see the infinite Creator of all revealed in the Messiah, Jesus. And we know our omnipotent God and our Messiah through His Word, the Bible.

The Bible, God's Word, is where He reveals His ways and purposes to us. It is the place where we come to know our Heavenly Father and Jesus, His Son. Hebrews 4:12 tells us, "For the word of God is living and powerful, and sharper than any two-edged sword, piercing even to the division of soul and spirit, and of joints and marrow, and is a discerner of the thoughts and intents of the heart."

This living, powerful sword (Ephesians 6:17) transforms and changes us, corrects and disciplines us, encourages and strengthens us. It teaches us to experientially know God. Throughout history, it was the people who knew their God who were strong and carried out great exploits (Daniel 11:32). These great men and women of faith were students of God's Word, spending time in it every day. They treated the

---

1. This incident resulted in our scratched, worn, hardwood floors being completely refinished and our never-quite-completed kitchen floor being marvelously redone and *finished!* Plus, while the work was being done, we were given a three-day vacation on the Oregon coast, courtesy of our homeowner's insurance! Thank You, Jesus!!!

Scriptures as infinitely more precious than a goldmine, finding the limitless treasures contained in it. And as they were transformed by the renewing of their minds, they made a tremendously significant impact on their world.

How do we fit personal Bible study into our already maximized schedule? That is an important and honest question that needs to be answered. For me, when our children were very young, it seemed a struggle to have a moment alone (even in the bathroom!!!). Ruth Bell Graham, wife of Billy Graham, experienced that same kind of difficulty in finding the opportunity to have a quiet time. In one of her books, she described a solution that worked for her when her children were little. On her window sill above the kitchen sink, she sat her Bible open to Proverbs so that she could, as she washed the dishes, glean morsels of truth for her family that day. That's a bit of down-to-earth reality! All of us do dishes at least once a day, don't we? Rather than complain about how we can't spend three hours a day reading the Bible (!), let's do what we can do. And as our children get older, those long, luxurious times with God may realistically become possible.

If we want to be really honest here, God showed me that I did manage to find time to read—books, newspapers, magazines—nearly every day. I was simply giving other things priority in my reading time. Edith Schaeffer, wife of Dr. Francis Schaeffer, brought this truth home to me in her books. She described coming to the growing conviction that if God was truly number one in her life, her reading ought to reflect it. So she made it a rule for herself to read the Bible first and to make sure that she read this most important book for at least the same amount of time as any other book. Whew! That will change your life! Forever!!

Though there are some tremendous books on Bible study, if this is a new and unfamiliar concept to you, let's take a spin through the essentials. First, to study the Bible, you need to read it. If your reading has been of the "start reading wherever it falls open" variety, let me encourage you to begin a systematic reading program. If you can, try to read at least one chapter per day, beginning with one of the Gospels in the New Testament. If you have a bit more time, add a chapter from the beginning of the Old Testament (Genesis). And to really encourage and strengthen yourself, add one chapter from Psalms or Proverbs.

Don't be overwhelmed. There are times when, with only a moment to read, I find a Scripture that I can "chew on" (think about, consider, meditate upon) throughout the day. To illustrate this, I once heard of a woman who spent her childhood years in a Godless, abusive home. As a young girl, she had to be up at the crack of dawn to work on her parents' farm. With only a few minutes to call her own each day, she would read a verse of Scripture and then memorize it. All day long, while working in the fields, she would recite the verse to herself and ponder it in her heart. As time went on, this growing young woman became known in her community for her deep devotion to the Lord and her profound knowledge of His Word. Her life and ministry were a testimony of the fact that God will work with what we have to give Him.

Second, to become students of the Word, we need to ponder and meditate on what we have read. It is not enough to read a certain number of verses, say "Amen," shut your Bible, and never give it another thought. When you read a verse like James 1:19–20, "So then, my beloved brethren, let every man be swift to hear, slow to speak, slow to wrath; for the wrath of man does not produce the righteousness of God," it is important to consider what you just read. The questions to ask yourself are, Does this apply to brothers only? (NO!) Does this apply only when dealing with adults? (NO!) Could this verse have anything to do with our parenting and our homeschool? (YES!) As you ponder this verse, ask God to show you whether at times you have been slow to hear, quick to speak, and quick to wrath. I have been guilty of this—well, more than once! Just as Jesus promised, the Holy Spirit convicts us concerning sin and guides us into all truth (John 15:8,13).

That brings us to the third essential of Bible study—applying what you have read to your own life. In our example, if you were confronted by your own lack of listening and anger toward the children, you would need to bring this to Jesus and ask forgiveness. "If we confess our sins, He is faithful and just to forgive us our sins and to cleanse us from all unrighteousness" (1 John 1:9). All means ALL!

Next, ask God to help you. Do you struggle with whether He's big enough to help, even in your situation? "Ah, Lord GOD! Behold, You have made the heavens and the earth by Your great power and outstretched arm. There is nothing too hard for You" (Jeremiah 32:17). And as I often tell my children, "Nothing means NOTHING!!!"

As we grow in our own Bible study time, we need to be teaching our children to have their own personal devotional time in the Word of God (when they are old enough to read). How? First, obviously, it makes a big difference whether or not we are doing it ourselves. [Diana's maxim: It is not what's taught but what's caught that counts.] Second, by reading and discussing the Bible together as a family on a regular basis, we demonstrate to our children how to approach the Bible—how to use good study aids, how to have good principles of interpretation, how to apply what we learn to our own lives.

It is such an incredible experience to have your child dash into your room, Bible in hand, yelling, "Mom, Mom! Look what I just discovered!!" I have always heard it said that God does not have grandchildren (we all need our own birth into His family), but it is unimaginably wonderful when God gives your children direct insight into His Word—without your help.

Prayer is the other dynamic of a growing relationship with God, since prayer is just a fancy name for talking and listening to the Lord. It's hard to get to know someone you never talk to. The amazing, incredible, mind-boggling thing about talking to God is that He always has time for you. Regardless of the other billions of people who may be talking to Him at the same moment, because He is infinite AND personal, God listens to *you*. In fact, the Scriptures indicate that He *never* uses an answering machine! "I'm sorry, God is not available right now, but if you leave your name and number after the beep, He'll get right back to you." That never, never, never happens! Psalm 139:17–18 says, "How precious also are Your thoughts to me, O God! How great is the sum of them! If I should count them, they would be more in number than the sand; when I awake, I am still with You."

Luxuriate in this understanding: you are loved immeasurably (John 3:16); God thinks of you more often than you can count (Psalm 139:17–18); He cares about you and your needs ("casting all your care upon Him, for He cares for you" 1 Peter 5:7); and He longs for the joy of spending time sharing with you ("O my dove, in the clefts of the rock, in the secret places of the cliff, let me see your countenance, let me hear your voice" Song of Solomon 2:14). So what are we waiting for?

Remember that prayer is both talking AND listening. How do you listen to God? There are many wonderful books about hearing and discerning the voice of God (one of my personal favorites is Loren Cunningham's *Is That Really You, God?*). To look briefly, though, at this important part of our relationship with God, it is important to realize that most often God speaks to His people through the Bible. As you are reading in the Scriptures, you will probably sometimes experience the sensation of having a verse jump out at you. Perhaps you have been praying about a decision to be made, when all of a sudden, a Scripture you've read a million times before is covered with blinking neon lights. You *know* that God has just spoken to you and has revealed the answer to your prayer.

Or, in your quiet times alone with God, you may suddenly remember an angry word you spoke that morning to your spouse or a midnight trip to the cookie jar you made a few days ago. Why does that thought pop into your mind right then? Probably because God is speaking to your heart. Knowing that unresolved conflict and unrepented sin will harm you, He gently brings these things to your conscience that you might get it right with Him and with others. Try 1 John 1:9. Confess this thing to God and experience the health-giving freshness of His forgiveness. [Caution: God, though He brings conviction, never brings condemnation! It is crucial to learn to tell the difference!!]

Other times, a quiet thought will suddenly come to you—an urge to pray for someone, or to telephone a family member, or to bake cookies for a new mom in your church. As we pay attention and follow through, we will begin to know that voice of God in our hearts. Remember, God will *never* speak to our hearts contrary to what Scripture says. That is one of the reasons it is so important to grow in our knowledge of the Bible.

In our family, we have found it helpful to have different kinds of prayer times. There are times when each of us prays alone, communicating the innermost thoughts of our heart to God and waiting upon Him; other times, Bill and I pray together, both in giving thanks and in bringing mutual concerns to Him; still other times, our entire family gathers for prayer.

If your children feel uncomfortable praying as a family, talk about it. Discuss what prayer is (talking to God in a natural manner), consider together the protocol of coming before the King of kings (Psalm 100:4 "Enter into His gates with thanksgiving, and into His courts with praise"), and explain how to be respectful of each other during prayer ("It's against the rules to throw things when someone is praying!") Then, just do it! It may take time to become comfortable with one another and familiar with the dynamics of family prayer. What will really light a fire under your family is to keep a prayer journal, recording what you pray for and the date God answers your prayer! Children become very motivated when they see that God really does listen and answer. "The effective, fervent prayer of a righteous man avails much" (James 5:16).

Minister to...My Neighbor?

Jesus said, "'You shall love the LORD your God with all your heart, with all your soul, and with all your mind.' This is the first and great commandment. And the second is like it: 'You shall love your neighbor as yourself.' On these two commandments hang all the Law and the Prophets" (Matthew 22:37–40).

We have been considering what it means as families and individuals to love the Lord. But how do families love their neighbor as themselves? Who *are* our neighbors, anyway? And how much time is this going to take? (After all, we have a homeschool schedule to keep and dinner to get on the table!)

Briefly, we need to not take on more than we can do. But there are things we *can* do even while we stay at home and teach our children. First, and most importantly, we can pray for people, both Christian and non-Christian—family, friends, neighbors, church members, government leaders, missionaries, victims of tragedies. We can also pray for our cities, our country, other countries, and for God's will to be done on earth as in heaven. If we had a clue how much impact our prayers have and how much they accomplish, we would not pooh-pooh the importance of this unseen ministry. We recently heard of a man who retired from his business so that he can spend several hours each day in prayer for missionaries. Prayer is important work, is worthy of our effort, and makes an eternal difference.

Beyond that, have a sensitive heart to the ways God may show you to love your neighbor. You may know someone who just had a baby or is recovering from an illness. Could your family prepare a wonderful, nutritious meal to deliver to this person? Are there elderly people in your family, in your church, or in your community who would benefit from regular visits? Perhaps you could "adopt" a shut-in and bring love and light into the person's life. This person may enjoy being an audience for your child's presentation, book report, or science project. You will be equally blessed if you become the audience for an elderly person's stories of former days.

We just learned of an elderly woman in our community who is a pen pal with a young homeschool girl who lives in our community. Mrs. Washburn is sharing pictures of horses that her daughter drew as a young girl with this budding artist, Katie Sowers. Katie has been encouraged by Mrs. Washburn to keep a journal of family events, like the funny things her siblings say: "Mommy, does milk talk?" All of this encouragement is taking place through the mail, though Katie makes occasional visits to take Mrs. Washburn homemade bread. What a wonderful, delightful idea.

What about helping folks move? Or participating in a barn raising? (Yes, they still do that in some places!) Or painting someone's house? Or pulling weeds in a garden? Or even cleaning the church? In our little church, every family pitches in and cleans once every few weeks. Our family has begun to take great delight in this chance to serve, and each of us has a special area of ministry. (Mine is the women's restroom!)

Your family may also have the opportunity to serve others in more radical ways. God may call you to open your home to an unwed mother. You may find yourselves helping in the local soup kitchen or marching in a right-to-life rally. God may direct your family to work in an inner-city ministry. There are many, many possibilities, especially as our children mature.

As Rob Gregory, formerly of Focus on the Family, said, we must not "circle the wagons." We need not become twentieth-century monks, content to maintain safety inside the four walls of our homes while the rest of the world goes to hell. Instead, our focus in homeschooling should be to raise spiritual, godly warriors prepared to do battle for people's souls—in God's way.

Finally, as God leads you, consider family missions. What if—just what if—part of His plan in bringing about the phenomenon of homeschooling is to strategically prepare His people to go out in tightly knit, healthy family units mobilized to share the good news around the world? It might not be tomorrow, but God could be placing a call to world missions on your family for the future.

Don't worry. If it's His call, He'll give the you desire AND make the way. But if you want to get started on preparing your family for a missions experience, you might want to do some reading on the subject. There are many excellent books on missions available (though not much about *family* missions). A fabulous series of fictional books on missions, targeted to children, is the *Reel Kids Adventures* by Dave Gustaveson. Having spent many years on foreign mission fields, Dave gives an authentic flavor to each of his books while providing a very realistic look at missions.

Your family is intrinsically important in the plan of God. Whether you are just beginning your family or whether all of your children are grown and out of the house, He has a plan for you. God's plan is specifically designed to fit just who you are and was established before the foundations of the world. Don't be content to settle for less when you can experience the wonder of living vitally for God. "For I know the plans I have for you, says the LORD, plans for good and not for evil, to give you a future and a hope" (Jeremiah 29:11). "We are His workmanship, created in Christ Jesus for good works" (Ephesians 2:10).

Recommended Reading

Children's Inductive Bible Study by Janice Southerland
> This homeschool mom was teaching Precept Bible Study Method to adults and wished it were available for her children. Not finding any suitable materials, she made her own. CIBS is thoughtfully prepared and carefully directed to the intellectual needs of second to fifth graders. We adapted it with tremendous success to our older children.

Is That Really You, God? by Loren Cunningham
Daring to Live on the Edge by Loren Cunningham
Winning God's Way by Loren Cunningham
> These three books, written by the founder of Youth With A Mission, are life changing! They explain how to personally know God's direction, His provision, and His ways. Written from decades of worldwide missionary service, they will encourage you in the adventures of faith.

Tracking Your Walk by Jim and Michelle Drake
> This wonderful book is a children's prayer journal. (You will need one for each of your children.) Because this is a creative and interesting format, it is an excellent tool to draw all of your children into penmanship, creative writing, geography, history, missions, Bible study, and prayer.

Reel Kids Adventures by Dave Gustaveson

    The Missing Video   *The Mysterious Case*

    Mystery at Smokey Mountain   *The Amazon Stranger*

    The Stolen Necklace   *The Dangerous Voyage*

    Exciting, can't-put-them-down, fictional accounts of modern-day missions adventures for children (I couldn't stop reading them, either).

Let Prayer Change Your Life by Becky Tirabassi

    A homeschooling friend in Michigan bought this book for me and said, "Read it! It'll change your prayer life!" I did, and it did. Very practical and easy to read, it encourages one to commit to daily prayer. It also contains excellent suggestions for creating a prayer notebook and organizer.

Concordance

Greek Lexicon

Bible Handbook

Expository Dictionary

    These are all tools of the trade for those who want to study their Bible seriously. Ask your Christian bookstore for help in selecting the best for your situation. Any of these resources will be one of the best investments you have ever made.

From Precepts Ministries, books by Kay Arthur

    Kay will help you really dig into a particular book of the Bible while asking questions that cause you to consider the application in your life of what you are learning. Excellent!

Chapter 12

෴

Blow Up the TV!

A few years ago, Monte and Karey Swan were the main speakers at a convention in Sioux Falls, South Dakota. As long-time homeschooling parents, they had many wonderful insights and experiences to share with the audience. But I think the thing that really stuck with us all was when Monte talked about television.

Monte described having come to the decision eighteen years previously to turn off what was essentially a time waster. Instead, he and his family spend time bow hunting, gardening on a mountainside, collecting an incredible library of old books, composing and singing music, reading great books, raising chickens, doing school, creating art (whether sculpture, painting, quilting, etc.), studying rocks (he is a professional geologist), and helping other families homeschool. They built their fantastically unique home themselves high up on a mountain in Colorado. In a word, these folks are doers.

Monte said that when people ask, "How on earth do you accomplish so much?", his reply is simple.

"I quit watching TV eighteen years ago. The four hours a day spent by average Americans watching television, times eighteen years NOT spent in front of the TV, means that I have had FOUR MORE YEARS than you to get things done."

Our Journal

It didn't happen all at once. Slowly but surely, by God's grace, we began to have better things to do with our time than sit in front of a television. The gradual replacement of that passive activity with things that were more interesting, more exciting, and more productive helped to wean this former television addict from her addiction to the point that one day, while visiting the home of some friends who had a television running continuously, I recognized a sense of absolute freedom from that idiot box.

If one removes the main source of interest from one's evenings and living room, what does one replace it with? We found that reading books out loud together was one of the most family-building activities we could do. We also discovered a real zest for game nights, singalongs, and swimming together at our local recreation center. In fact, we now often bemoan the fact that we don't have MORE time to have a quiet evening reading at home.

A few years ago we began reading *Anne of Green Gables* by Lucy Maud Montgomery to our children in the evening. With more than my share of "ham," I read Anne's conversations with others in a sort of nonstop, breathlessly enthusiastic, wildly optimistic way. As we read of her volatile confrontations with those who mocked her red hair, peals of laughter erupted around the room. When we watched Anne—with hair dyed green because of her failed attempt to make herself "beautiful"—pay the penalty for her behavior by having to stay home until her hair grew out, we laughed, and then, more soberly, we talked about reaping what you sow. When, at last, Matthew, her beloved adopted uncle, had heart failure and died, we all cried. Bill was able, haltingly, to share with us his own deeply felt childhood heartache over the death of his grandfather.

We grew together as a family as we came to know this other family through the pages of a book. It deepened our understanding of each other as we shared together and increased our awareness of the realities of life as we laughed and cried over the events in Anne's life. Reading that book together changed us.

As our habit of reading together has grown, we've started finding things for our hands to do while our ears and hearts listen. While Bill reads, I crochet or knit, Isaac draws, Melody paints or colors, and Michael works on leather or wood. Not only does this allow for many "finished-at-last" projects, it also allows a deeper sense of fulfillment in each of us. No one is sitting idle, all are happily creating, and though we do different things, we do them together.

Sometimes our reading aloud takes place when someone is making dinner or doing dishes or baking cookies. Often we read books aloud as we travel in the car. There are times when Michael and Melody take turns reading a series of books to each other (like the *Adventures in the Northwoods* by Lois Walfrid Johnson); Isaac and Michael also take turns reading books to each other (like WWII adventure stories); Bill is reading still another book to Melody (a missionary story), while I read *God's Smuggler* by Brother Andrew out loud to the boys; Bill reads out loud to me while I cook, and I read excerpts to him from books we enjoy.

The more you share in the adventures of reading great books out loud, the more you will *want* to do it. (It's kind of like eating a potato chip—it's hard to stop at one!) And I guarantee you, the growing sense of family togetherness cannot be found in any box—not even a 26-inch, color, surround sound, cable-ready box.

Quality Family Time—Just Do It!

OK. You're convinced. Your brand-new 26-inch television is in the garage sale pile. The three-year-old television is hooked up only to the VCR so that when the mood strikes, your family can watch *The Sound of Music.* The mini black and white TV you used to have in your kitchen was donated to a nursing home. Now what?!

Learn from the Boy Scouts: Be Prepared. When you hear "Mommmmmmm, how am I going to know what happens on my favorite show?" "Daddddddd, what's there to do?" "Honeyyyyyy, quick, help me—I feel a television urge coming over me!" have something exciting and wonderful on hand to offer.

"Let's drive up to the canyon and hike along the riverside." "Let's start a round-robin tournament of dominoes." "I just checked these fabulously funny books out of the library. We're going to read 'em and weep...er, I mean, laugh!" "Let's visit that new homeschooling family." "I just bought passes for our whole family to that new recreation center—let's go for a swim."

New patterns and habits take time to develop. But if you persevere and if you pray for God's wisdom and mercy, they will develop.

Picture it like this. For years you have been buying white bread at the grocery store—not the white bread with all kinds of nutritious things added, but the plain old, unimpressive, cheap white bread that is composed of mostly air and sawdust. New friends move in next door and you notice how healthy and vibrant they all are. When you ask the reason for their great vitality, they tell you, "Oh, we grind our own wheat and make fresh bread from it every day." When you look at your own pale, tired, worn-to-a-frazzle couch potatoes, you decide to ask your neighbors for help in learning how to bake bread. They set you up with fifty pounds of wheat, a secondhand wheat grinder, a bread machine that does it all, and an electric knife to cut the fragrantly wonderful bread. Guess what? No matter how marvelous that 100 percent whole wheat bread is, it is going to take time for your family to develop an appreciation for it. But is it worth it? Absolutely! Just look at your imaginary neighbors' kids to see the difference it will make in your own children's lives. Will it happen eventually? Absolutely!

The principle of reaping what you sow permeates our entire world. If you sow good things, you will reap good results; if you sow bad, worthless, wasteful things, you will reap bad, worthless, wasteful results. (Remember, though, as any farmer will tell you, there is a healthy bit of time between sowing and reaping.) So let us sow Philippians 4:8:

> Finally, brethren, whatever things are true, whatever things are noble, whatever things are just, whatever things are pure, whatever things are lovely, whatever things are of good report, if there is any virtue and if there is anything praiseworthy—meditate on these things.

All right. How and what do we sow? How do we unplug the worthless and plug in the true, noble, just, pure, lovely, good, virtuous, and praiseworthy? The list of possibilities is nearly endless and will be as unique as your own family. Here is a list of some of our favorites. Following the list are some descriptive explanations of each item.

- ⌒ Read out loud together.
- ⌒ Do physical activities together.
- ⌒ Share something new together.
- ⌒ Pass on your heritage.
- ⌒ Sing and make music together.
- ⌒ Laugh together!

∾ Read out loud together. Excellent stories are available for all interests and levels. Classics have served well for generations, and new books of exceptional quality are being written every day. There are some wonderful books about books that will get you started. Gladys Hunt's books *Honey for a Child's Heart* and *Read for Your Life – Turning Teens into Readers* are both fabulous resources. *Books Children Love* by Elizabeth Wilson is one of my favorite books for learning about the tremendous variety of books available in different subject areas. Ask your local librarian for other resources that describe which books are good for reading out loud.

Here are my top ten tips for reading out loud:

(1) Choose books you yourself loved as a child.

(2) Select books with humor as much as possible. That will keep everyone interested and tuned in.

(3) Read with as much dramatic flair as possible. It helps to let the person who has this gifting be the actor/actress—your spouse or one of your older children might become the "designated reader" of your family.

(4) Don't read past the point of no return. If folks are falling asleep, yawning, or fidgeting too much, stop! [Diana's maxim: It is far better to leave them hanging than to leave them sleeping.]

(5) Set reasonable goals for reading out loud. If your children are six and under, don't try to read Tolstoy's *War and Peace* to them. But if your children are older, stretch them a bit.

(6) If a book turns out to be too difficult or uninteresting to your family, close it! [Diana's maxim: Kicking a dead horse doesn't get you anywhere.]

(7) As much as is possible, maintain a regular time of reading out loud. It is not efficient to start a book and then set it down for three weeks before resuming it. Whether you can read five nights a week, three nights a week, or one night a week, try to set and keep a routine.

(8) It is "legal" to read for great periods of time if the story is captivating to the entire family. As I was reading another Anne of Green Gables book, we came to a part that was absolutely impossible to find a stopping place. I read on and on and on, as my children begged, "Please, please, DON'T STOP!", until we finished the last page. It was 12:30 a.m., but it was a special—never to be recaptured—moment in our family. (And we slept in the next morning!)

(9) Variety, as they say, is the spice of life. Find different topics, different styles, different authors, different historic periods of time to read about.

(10) Remember the point of this endeavor—building a shared sense of togetherness. Be sensitive to the likes and dislikes of *all* the members of your family, even if it means reading *Hank, The Cowdog* because that is the only book everyone enjoys.[1]

⤖ Do physical activities together. Walk together, bike together, hunt together, skate together, hike together, swim together, fish together, wrestle—well, whoever wants to...I always leave the room!—clog dance together, camp together, ski together, etc., etc., etc.

There is something profoundly wonderful about being in God's nature together. It not only develops muscles and skill, it also develops a closeness and a bonding in our families. And many of the things to do on this list are free!

One October, we had the unbelievable opportunity to camp for a few days in a motor home on a nearly deserted beach on the Oregon coast. There was nothing between us and the waves of the pounding Pacific except for a few grains of sand. In this majestic, breathtaking arena we met a homeschooling family that lived nearby. Allen and Cheryl Walz and their three children owned part of the campground and were some of the most delightful people we have ever had the chance to know. They were unique in many ways, but one of the most amazing was the twice-daily hike they took across the beach and across the hills of their property. Rain or shine, blustery or calm, they packed up their three children and walked several miles per day. It was a time to be out in God's creation, a time to exercise, a time to pray, and a time to talk about what was in their hearts. And it was a marvelous, relation-building time for their family.

We know lots of homeschooling families who camp regularly. (I'm sorry to disappoint you, but this is not my cup of tea. My idea of roughing it is when the motel has no pool!) Other families, though, relate to us their enjoyment in the adventures of camping, hunting, or fishing together.

---

1. We started reading the *Hank, The Cowdog* series by John Erickson because of someone's recommendation. Though it doesn't stretch the mind at all and has no great moral to the story, it has provided some of the most hilarious laughter of our family's whole-born-put-together.

Probably the most amazing "living it up in the wild" homeschooling friends we have are Dan and Koleen Ingalls (distant relatives of Laura Ingalls Wilder). Dan and Koleen are cattle ranchers in Wyoming and are raising six boys. They have been homeschooling for years and have very special sons to show for it. In the summer, they move their cows and their kids up to the Teton Mountains. They spend the entire summer grazing cows, watching for grizzlies (gulp!), riding horses, hunting and fishing, cooking, and doing chores in the great outdoors. Then in October, they trail their cows home (as in, real-life cowboying!). So, now, you have a real camper/hunter/fisher's goal to shoot for!

∘━∘ Share something new together. If you develop a family interest in a hobby, project, craft, etc., your children will soon have something better than television to be interested in. Perhaps this new interest will develop into a part-time business for budding entrepreneurs!

Though we are all different, with different tastes, here are a few suggestions: woodworking, dried flower arranging, photography, raising chickens, making cheese, creating new flavors of ice cream (I know, it's a messy job, but *somebody* has to do it!), growing herbs in pots for an herb garden, making dollhouses complete with furnishings and handmade rugs, tackling increasingly difficult jigsaw puzzles (I once saw one that was all white!), reciting Shakespeare, or studying opera.

For our family, our latest new shared interest is learning about opera. It all started with the *Barber of Seville* by Rossini. The music is so much fun, the storyline is so crazy (similar to Shakespeare's impossible-situation comedies), and we all love trying to sing, "Figaro, Figaro, Figaro" as fast as the baritone does. From this easy-to-enjoy beginning, we are working our way into more difficult operas. Why? I don't know, except that the music is so incredible and because it is so much fun to share something new as a family. As I said, we are all different. (Some of us are more different than others!!)

∘━∘ Pass on your heritage, your knowledge, your passions to your children. How many times have you met someone whose parents spoke a language other than English but did not teach their children their mother tongue? Most of the children, when grown, lament the fact that they did not learn their parents' language, feeling that a part of their heritage was missing.

In our age of private lessons, team sports, and cultural endeavors, it is very easy to lose sight of our need to give our children what is in our own lives. We think we're giving them the best when we run them to ballet lessons, violin lessons, swimming lessons, and bicycle seat repair class.

But there is only a certain amount of time in each person's life, and to choose to spend your time doing one thing means that you do not have the time to do something else. So what is the most important element to give our children? What deserves the priority of time? I believe we need to give them the heritage that is in our life first.

An example of this is in my own kitchen. Having been raised on Mexican food, Chinese food, East Indian food, seafood, Italian food, and German food, my tastebuds developed some rather unusual appreciations for ethnic cooking. As a French major in college, I learned to prepare foods à la français by spending time with French people. Encouraged by success, I began learning to cook all of my ethnic favorites from childhood. You must understand, this was pure bliss to me! There was nothing quite so magnificent as whipping up a batch of Chinese egg rolls, or coq au vin, or shrimp curry. While my children were still very young, I taught ethnic cooking classes, sort of a local Galloping Gourmet, with lots of laughter and lots of food. Many people hired me to cater special occasions for them, and it was so much fun to create new taste sensations.

A few years ago it dawned on me that my children knew nothing about how to cook (beyond the Kraft macaroni & cheese level). The Lord gently confronted me with my own selfishness. Yes, it takes a lot longer to show someone else how to do something than to do it yourself. Yes, there is a bigger mess in the kitchen when children are involved (though my husband tells me that *no one* makes a bigger mess than I do when I am catering). Yes, it requires effort, energy, and a willingness to share to teach your children how to create culinary masterpieces. But isn't an important part of parenting to pass on what is important to you? And if you don't do it, who will?

As we've stayed in other homeschooling families' homes, we have seen parents passing on such skills as quilting, gardening, sewing, woodworking, auto mechanics, music, cooking, computer (though that is often a case of children teaching their parents), business, decorating, flying airplanes, and writing. What's in *your* life to pass on to *your* children?

∽ Sing and make music together. Even though this was mentioned in a previous chapter, it is worth considering again. Back in the days before tape players, CDs, boom boxes, televisions, radios, and stereos, people usually created their own entertainment. Family singalongs, hymn sings, instrumentals, hoedowns, and square dances all contributed to the sense of community and to the sense of family fun. Now, with all of our high-tech quality, we are missing the satisfaction and fun of do-it-yourself music.

One of my Hear & Learn partners, John Standefer, spent his childhood in Texas. He describes the entire family sitting on the porch during the evenings, making music on a variety of instruments, reading portions of the Bible, and singing together. That is where he got his start as a musician. It was a safe place to try different instruments and an encouraging place to experiment with different musical techniques. But more than that, as John relates this part of his childhood, it is with a deep appreciation for the family memories.

Our family has for the past few years been learning songs from the Civil War era, along with sea chanteys from the tall ships and whalers. When we are working together setting up an exhibit at a convention, it is fairly common for one of us to lead out in a song and the rest to join in heartily. It is fun, it is infectious, and it builds a sense of belonging. Though we are sometimes slightly off-key, we oftentimes forget the words, and we don't always agree on how to end the song, it is still definitely worthwhile. As my music teacher used to tell me, "Practice makes perfect!"

Will you try? Will you open this musical door a little bit? Will you give your family the opportunity to share in this richness together, however imperfectly? Try singing along with recordings first, then go it alone later on. If there is some hesitancy on the part of your children, start with funny songs—people are supposed to laugh during them anyway.

ᜤᜨ Laugh together. After all, homeschooling *is* a laughing matter. Proverbs tells us that a "merry heart does good like a medicine." If we cultivate humor in our home, it will have a healthy effect on all the inhabitants.

Since the surrounding culture does not provide good models for humor (to say the least!), we realized that we needed to set up rules for godly humor in the family. Here they are:

I. The Rules of The "Good Humor" Family

A. Do NOT gain a laugh at someone else's expense. Tell jokes on your own foibles, but don't capitalize on the weak spots of others.

B. Put-down humor is *not* funny and is not allowed.

C. Sarcasm is not humor. In fact, the Greek stem of "sarcasm" means to "tear flesh!" And that is exactly what it does to the victim. Sarcasm and snide remarks are half-truths veiled as clever comments.

They breed misunderstanding and carry great offense. The law of love disqualifies them for parents or children.

D. Puns are worth mastering. "That is an "egg"cellent pun… Oh, I don't know. It seems a little cracked to me!"

E. Memorize a few good jokes, then add to collection. Here is my all-time favorite: "What did the Spanish fireman name his twin sons?" "José and Hose B!"

With the rules firmly enforced, play with humor. It is a skill that needs to be cultivated, and it takes practice. As a family, we are safe to make mistakes, to fail, to tell a "groaner." In fact, the family is the only safe place to learn how to be funny.

One of the best ways to develop humor in your family is through reading funny literature. This might range from *101 Elephant Jokes* (my copy is about thirty years old, but it still *is* funny!) to *The Comedy of Errors* by William Shakespeare. You could read funny poetry, joke books, books of puns, and funny classic literature. We love Victor Borge's videos (combining classical music and humor). We have listened to *old* audio recordings of funny comics, like vintage Bill Cosby and Dick Newhart. [Caution: Because of the changing morals in our culture, comic routines of the past several years have degenerated considerably, even among Christian comics, some of whom seem to have ignored the law of love. If someone in the family finds an old recording of a comic, Mom and Dad need to listen to it first to make sure it has nothing objectionable.]

The more your family develops its funny bone, the more you will all laugh. And the more you laugh, the more you will see the humor in situations. One day, I was beginning to read Isaac the riot act for leaving bread out on the counter. All of a sudden I realized that I had to look up to him!!! (These changes happen suddenly, without fanfare or notice.) It was suddenly hysterically funny to me that I was having to raise my face to get in his! We both burst out laughing at the same time! Discipline around our house, since I have lightened up, has cheerfully never been the same. So… LAUGH!

Recommended Reading

The Child Influencer's by Dan Adams
An excellent exposé concerning the influence of television, peers, and schools. After reading this book, you'll

be convinced that homeschooling and discarding the television are the very best things you can do for your children.

Reader's Digest Children's Songbook
> A great collection of songs for families.

History Alive! Through Music—America by Diana Waring
History Alive! Through Music—Westward Ho! by Diana Waring
History Alive! Through Music—Musical Memories of Laura Ingalls Wilder by Bill Anderson
> A fun, singable, informative selection of American folk songs. The history behind each song is included in the accompanying book, along with guitar chords and melody lines.

Tom Glazer's Treasury of Folk Songs for Children by Tom Glazer
> Probably my favorite collection of children's songs—though hard to find.

Off the Church Wall by Rob Portlock
Way Off the Church Wall by Rob Portlock
> A humorous look through the art of cartooning at church life. We have laughed, grinned, and groaned our way through these books several times.

101 Elephant Jokes compiled by Robert Blake
> Our edition is 1964, so you can imagine how dog-eared it is! However, these silly jokes and puns never lose their appeal—they cycle periodically through our conversations to the hilarity of all.

Joke books by Bob Philips
> Mr. Philips has several joke books that are funny, appropriate, and usable in the quest to teach our children humor. One day I read several pages of jokes out loud to Bill, and by the end, I could barely get the words out because of uncontrollable laughter on my part. (Sometimes these things build up on you, you understand!)

Chapter 13

❦

Creating an Atmosphere
Or,
Beauty and the Best

*I*t was a place of unspeakable beauty. The antique table settings glistened in the candlelight while the rich darkness of wood reflected the glow of lights from around the room. Each of those participating in the sumptuous feast set before them could only marvel at the delicacies, at the intricately fashioned flavors, at the stunning beauty of the presentation. It was the most amazing dinner of my life.

We had come to Chalet Suzanne in Lake Wales, Florida, at the invitation of Bob and Tina Farewell. The meticulously kept grounds of the chalet were also the grounds of Bob and Tina's home and business, so to visit one was to visit the other. Our family had spent several enjoyable days sharing ideas, reading books, laughing together, discussing experiences. As our time together drew to a close, Bill and I were invited by another couple to dine at the chalet. Having never before eaten at a four-star restaurant, I waited in great anticipation for that evening to arrive.

As the day sank into twilight, the lights on the chalet transformed this lovely building into a fairyland castle. From the moment we entered the restaurant, we were ushered into an atmosphere of antique beauty, of meticulous care for details, of attentive service, of wonderful creativity spilling out into every corner, and to the most marvelous foods I had ever eaten. It was a magical, perfect evening whose memory I gratefully savour now and again.

The following day, Tina took me through the back door of the chalet to the kitchen and preparation areas. I was allowed to poke my nose into every nook and cranny (a cook's delight!) and to observe the kitchen staff at their tasks. Do you know what I saw? Cans of tomato sauce, jars of mayonnaise, lettuce, meat, tomatoes, milk, grapefruit, cheese—nothing unusual, nothing magical, nothing that I wouldn't find in anyone's kitchen. What a shock! And what a blessing! You see, it wasn't the ingredients that made the difference—the ingredients were normal, common, and available to all. The real difference was in how creatively and skillfully the ingredients were prepared. And when the foods were ready to be served, they were not slapped carelessly onto a chipped plate. Instead, each portion was conscientiously placed on an artistically stunning plate with an eye for symmetry, beauty, and design. Though originating with the everyday and the ordinary, ingredients at Chalet Suzanne were thoroughly transformed into world-class, four-star meals through creative, thoughtful preparation and beautiful, artistic presentation.

Our Journal

About a year ago we met a family in Maine who celebrated Jewish-style Sabbath dinners. A few months later I spoke with a woman on the phone who shared that her family had also started keeping the Day of Rest with Sabbath dinners. This past spring, several families in our church thought it would be wonderful to hold a Passover Seder dinner, so I pulled out some books that we had collected over the years concerning Jewish feasts. Since each of these books listed "Sabbath Dinners" in the table of contents, I curiously read the descriptions of these weekly family celebrations. Finally, last summer we picked up a book entirely concerned with the keeping of the Sabbath.

For several years we had tried to hold Sundays as special, as days of rest (after the hustle and bustle of getting five of us to church!), as a time of being together and being with the Lord. What we were now hearing and reading, though, went much deeper. The experience of celebrating the Sabbath together as a family, starting with a special dinner the evening before, sounded richer, fuller, and more satisfying. So with a bit of trepidation, I announced to our children that we were going to try having a Sabbath dinner. My children, having heard from their friends in

Maine about how much fun these dinners were, gladly voiced their approval. In fact, they asked if they could help.

Everything we had read about Sabbath dinners indicated that they were a time of festivity—of special foods, flowers, candlelight, music, tablecloths, and china. I planned a dinner of French food (crêpes, not fries!). The children helped set the table with our china that previously had been used only at Christmas and for *really* special company. We got out the silverware inherited from my grandmother, and the children folded the cloth napkins in elegant style. Two brand-new white candles adorned the table, with a glass rose sitting between them. After putting the finishing touches to the meal, we all hurried to "dress" for dinner. Bill selected a beautiful symphony for our dinner music, and we were all set.

As we stood around our beautifully decorated table, with the glow of candlelight illuminating the scene, each dressed in his or her Sunday best, we experienced a profound sense of amazement and satisfaction that this bounteous celebration was all created just for us. And the sense of "special" pervaded the entire evening. We focused the conversation around the dinner table on the wonderful things God had been doing in our lives and on precious dreams for the future that had not yet been shared. A feeling of belonging, of togetherness, of being family gradually stole over us. We ended our first Sabbath dinner together reading out loud from a special book.

That was several months ago, and we have endeavored to continue this new tradition each week. A new consciousness of beauty and peace has entered our lives as the loveliness of the Sabbath spills out onto the other six days of the week. Our children are now experiencing regularly the specialness that had normally been reserved for company, and it is building a deeper sense of creativity and beauty in our family. Nothing else has ever contributed as much to the sense of God's blessing, His abundance, on us.

Homeschoolers Are Beautiful People!

If you are wondering what on earth a chapter on creativity and beauty is doing in a book about homeschooling, suffice it to say that "All work and no play make Jack and Jill pretty dull!" We can become so immersed in the never-ending rounds of laundry, cooking, chores, spelling assignments, shopping, correcting grammar, mending, refereeing squabbles, and quickly studying up on the next person in history that life can become rather gray and uninteresting. I believe that with a little thought and effort, our family's lives can be touched with beauty and enriched through creativity. The rewards will far outweigh the costs.

Everything in this chapter is presented as merely food for thought, as ideas you might consider for the reward they bring. If you are a beginning homeschooler still wondering how to teach phonics and get dinner on the table in the same day, relax. This is not a lecture on guilt or an expectation that your home will be featured in the Sunday newspaper. It is simply a chance to share an area that has enriched our lives and made the grind seem less like a grind and more like a delight. Perhaps after chewing on this for a while you will be encouraged to buy some candles and treat your family to the wonder of dinner by candlelight. Wonderful! From small beginnings come great things. And in our cultural setting, a family dinner enjoyed together over candlelight is no small accomplishment.

If the question lingers, Why take the time to make things look nice, what's the big deal about beauty anyway?, let us go all the way back to the One who originated the idea in the first place. Psalm 27:4 states: "One thing I have desired of the LORD, that will I seek: that I may dwell in the house of the LORD all the days of my life, to behold the beauty of the LORD, and to inquire in His temple."

The reason there is beauty in our world is that the Creator of all things thought it was worthwhile. That's quite a recommendation! Somehow, in expressing His creative thoughts, He not only gave us the plants, animals, rocks, and water needed for life but also made them utterly beautiful (some more so than others!). It could have all been absolutely utilitarian, practical, boring, gray, tasteless, uninteresting. But that is *not* how He did it.

In the beginning, when God said, "Let there be," He created a universe filled with beauty. Can you imagine? He started with absolutely nothing, a blank canvas, an empty stage. And then He began to lavishly create, using all the colors of the spectrum (which He also created). Have you ever wondered why there are so many shades of green or red or blue? I have, especially when trying to match paints! It is because of God's wonderful variety in creation. What about all the shapes and textures and sizes, from rugged mountains to the downy fuzz of a baby chick? Or consider the myriad of flavors He created—everything from nutmeg to jalapeños! What about all the different sounds we hear in nature? The majestic roar of the ocean, the raucous cry of the crow, the mysterious call of whales are all part of the amazingly diverse, awesomely beautiful creation of our God. Picture your absolute favorite setting in nature, whether mountaintop, ocean shore, desert, or forest. All these things that cause us to cry, "Oh, how beautiful!" are because of God's infinite creativity and His perfectly artistic eye for beauty. The unfathomable loveliness we see reflected in nature—even though it lost its perfection after the fall of man and groans in anticipation of redemption—remains breathtaking. The beauty of nature is merely a glimpse of the creative beauty of our God. Ecclesiastes 3:11 says, "He has made everything beautiful in its time."

One incredible aspect of the good news of Jesus is found in Isaiah 61:3: "to give them beauty for ashes, the oil of joy for mourning, the garment of praise for the spirit of heaviness." WE are the "them" being talked about. As we receive new birth into the family of God through the salvation of Jesus, He gives us His beauty instead of the dirty ashes we have been lugging around. Just think! It is a real, true-to-life Cinderella story! Jesus was revealed as our heavenly Prince as He rescued us from the ashes, took away the filthy rags of our own attempts to be good, and clothed us with His own robes of righteousness. We have been brought into the family of God, so we know the ending, "And they lived happily ever after" will be true throughout eternity. God not only created beauty but also bestows His beauty upon His children.

God's beauty, however, goes far beyond what the eye can see. His beauty works from the inside out. It is not that our faces or bodies are suddenly turned into those of Miss or Mr. America, but God works His beauty in us from the inside to the outside. This is not in the beauty of facial features or the latest hairdo but in piety and righteousness. 1 Chronicles 16:29 states, "Worship the LORD in the beauty of holiness!" It is His holiness, as we live in it, that makes *us* beautiful.

God is beautiful, and He has given us His beauty. What is our response? We are the children of the God who created everything. The Bible tells us that we are created in His image, and as we look around, it is obvious that part of being created in His image means that we have been endowed with the ability to also be creative. As Christians in a personal relationship with God Himself, we need to reflect His beauty in our lives, our families, and our homes—because we *know* Him.

Why creative beauty in our homes? Why, with all our hectic schedules and day-to-day demands, should we take on a further concern for beauty? Because God lives in us. As God places His own essence and nature within us, we will begin to reflect "from glory to glory" God's beauty, both in appreciation and in creation. God lavished beauty on His creation and in His temple (see 2 Chronicles 3:6). Therefore, we have a model for expressing creative beauty in our homes.

Many people, though they do not know the Lord, create amazing artistic beauty. How much more, then, should we, as the Creator's children, express beauty in our lives? It is *not* the same as sharing the gospel with an unbeliever, but committing to beauty *could* open a door as you exchange gardening ideas and flower bed designs with your next-door neighbor or as your guests feel refreshed just from being in your home. And remember, "whatever you do in word or deed, do all in the name of the Lord Jesus" (Colossians 3:17).

This is certainly not a suggestion that we all run out and build houses fancy enough to be featured in *House Beautiful*. Nor is it an indication that we need to hire an interior decorator to redo our homes. (Aren't you glad?!!) The kind of creative, expressive beauty I am speaking of can be as inexpensive as a packet of flower seeds. It can be changing the arrangement of the furniture in your living room to take better advantage of the garden view. It could, and probably should, begin with tidying up the living space. (Ouch!) The point is that creating beauty, regardless of how simple, has an important place in our lives and will, to some degree, reflect the Creator of all.

How on earth do we, as homeschoolers trying to do everything else demanded of us, take on yet another responsibility? I really think that it is not so much adding another job but simply enriching the one we already naturally do. Creating beauty can be as simple as setting candles on the table and lighting them for dinner, since the table has to be set for dinner anyway. If you are planning a garden to save on food costs for next winter, beauty could be as simple as adding a planting of columbine and forget-me-nots on the border of your vegetables. If you love to sew and have some pretty, durable material from the remnant section, fashion a lovely, homemade barrette for your daughter's hair in the same colors as the new dress you just made for her. If your family, as ours, serves meatless meals during the week to save money, beautify the serving of scalloped potatoes with green beans and beets, or sauteed mushrooms and fresh tomato slices, allowing the vivid colors to enhance the flavors. Beauty is choosing to spend four dollars of your food budget money for a bouquet of flowers from the local grocery store so that you can arrange them in an old-fashioned vase at home. It is crocheting a lovely doily to set under the pot of African violets, fashioning a pillow from velveteen scraps and lace to match the colors in your couch, or making a fragrant wreath for your kitchen with eucalyptus leaves, cinnamon sticks, and dried flowers. As in the story of Chalet Suzanne, we all have many of the same ingredients in our lives. It is what we do with them that makes the beautiful difference.

A life-changing book on this subject—I know…it changed mine—is Edith Schaeffer's *The Hidden Art of Homemaking*. Because Mrs. Schaeffer writes from such a rich experience of living "as unto the Lord," her thoughts both stretch and encourage us. Her suggestions are not pie in the sky. We can see the practical reality of what is being described, but we can also see the vast horizon of what might be if we try. The author takes us from where we all are into the possibilities of what can be done with what God has given us. *Hidden Art* is all about the creativity and beauty possible within such areas as music, gardening, flower arranging, sewing, food preparation, writing, drawing, and drama. Mrs. Schaeffer's book is the one that encouraged me to care what our dinner table looks like. We try to incorporate nice settings, not so I can hold up my nose and be a snob, but so our family can be blessed with a beautiful atmosphere. In an atmosphere of beauty, people feel special, conversations are encouraged, and relations develop. (We have not as yet attained to perfection in this. Just thought I'd make that clear in case you dropped in for tea someday!!)

Pass It On

OK. God created the beauty we see, He makes us beautiful through Jesus, and we reflect His beauty to those around us. How then, do we pass on this richness to our children? How do we encourage them in their fledgling attempts to follow Mom in her creativity?

Children need a safe atmosphere for experimenting with creativity and beauty in the same way that they need freedom for developing humor. Our homes need to become a safe haven for the imperfect attempts at trying something new. I am reasonably sure da Vinci did not paint a masterpiece on his first try, and it would be very interesting to see Michelangelo's first sculpture. It takes time, practice, and encouragement to develop skill in creativity, so we need to allow for mistakes and bloopers and blobs of paint on the kitchen table.

A good rule to follow is to not berate someone's artistic endeavor, especially during the first critical moments after creation. Though it is possible to offer helpful, constructive criticism, be careful to wait until the first blush of creativity has worn off. And when we offer constructive criticism, we need to remember to phrase it in a very positive manner. (Do you know the Rule of Sandwich? Always sandwich a criticism between two very affirming, supportive comments.)

There is nothing more defeating or humiliating than to have someone remark about one's newly created crayon masterpiece, "Brother, is that ugly!" or "Well, it would have been OK except that you used the wrong color" or "That is the stupidest looking picture I ever saw." Unfortunately, it is altogether too common to hear such comments, even among Christian parents. Then we excuse ourselves because we feel tired or hungry or stressed. My dear brothers and sisters, these things ought not to be so!

We need to nurture budding attempts at creativity, not squash them. Can you imagine how ridiculous it would be for a farmer who planted corn seed to wait impatiently for the harvest? What if the moment a little corn plant poked its tiny head out of the ground, the farmer yanked it out by its roots and stomped on it because it did not yet have a corncob? There would be precious little harvest from that farmer's field!

It takes time, time, and more time to gain skill—even in something as simple as folding cloth napkins properly. When your children help produce an atmosphere of beauty by creating a centerpiece for the table, encourage their beginnings—even if a bouquet of dandelions is not quite what you had in mind. When they fashion a little fan out of some old wallpaper samples, you could add leftover bits of lace to stimulate their further creative efforts. (Melody made literally dozens of these fans one year. Our pastor's wife, in an act of extreme creativity, fashioned a wall hanging of them for her guest room. It turned out to be absolutely beautiful, and everytime we visit their house, Melody is reminded of her own inventive hand in creating this work of art.)

I must confess to you, I often fail miserably in this area. Forgetting the Rule of Sandwich, I sometimes see only an imperfect attempt and criticize my children, who have often had to forgive Mom for her perfectionist tendencies. A principle Edith Schaeffer shares in many of her books deals with this: If you demand perfection or nothing, you will end up with nothing. Even if we sometimes fail because we demand perfection, we need to constantly remind ourselves to be gracious and to tolerate imperfection while we anticipate improvements.

Trying to create something of beauty is an act of vulnerability. When one is vulnerable, something wonderful is shared between creator and audience. A giving of oneself takes place in a very real sense, and we are allowed to have a glimpse inside another person's being. But to be vulnerable opens up the possibility of being deeply hurt. Therefore, we need as much as possible to establish an atmosphere of safety and acceptance that allows and protects the vulnerable expressions of our children, our spouses, and ourselves.

We are all dealing with this issue, whether we realize it or not. If we realize it and make a commitment to nurture creativity, something wonderful will happen. If we don't realize it, don't make time for it, and demand perfection from our children, something will die or be hardened inside of them. Being at home together, we have so many opportunities for living this out. To be careful to appreciate our children"s attempts at creativity is one of the most precious gifts we can give our children in homeschooling. We are their very best audience!

How many times have you heard, "Mommy, look what I made?" Even though what they hold out to you might be an unrecognizable creature of indeterminate color, this is the moment to say something affirming, positive, and affectionate. "Wow! I have never seen such an interesting drawing! You are *really* being creative today, honey! Can you tell Mommy who this is?" Be prepared! They just might lovingly reply, "You!"

Recommended Reading

The Hidden Art of Homemaking by Edith Schaeffer
> One of the most important books written on the subject of incorporating beauty into our everyday lives. I recommend that you buy it and then read it at least once a year!

What is a Family? by Edith Schaeffer
> This was *the* book that changed my understanding of family. Because of Mrs. Schaeffer's transparency, we are given a glimpse into a Christian family's relationships with one another. We see the reality of working through the difficulties and unfulfilled expectations that we *all*

experience from living in a fallen world. But we also see the great joys, rewards, and blessings of family life lived in commitment to each other, which is the motivation that keeps us going. I recommend, again, that you buy it and read it at least once a year! Better yet, buy two and pass one on!!

Books on
    Interior decoration
    Flower design
    Sewing
    Arts & crafts
    Cooking

Chapter 14

⟨ɷɯɯ૭⟩

Forever
Family Friendships

*J*osh and Cindy Wiggers, along with their three children, are hospitable people. We first met them at a homeschooling convention in Loveland, Colorado, when their booth "Geography Matters" was across the aisle from ours. My children spent most of that convention in the Wiggerses' booth because of all the fascinating maps, atlases, Geo-Safari games, and especially the hats and coats made from world maps. Bill and I took turns dashing over to visit with Josh and Cindy throughout the weekend, discovering that they were "good people."

As several more opportunities came for us to spend time with the Wiggers family at other conventions, the couple's wonderful relationship with each other became increasingly evident. We always observed lots of laughter, words of encouragement, and obvious interest in what the other thought in the interaction between these two. We greatly anticipated the joy that we would share when we accepted their offer to bunk at their house during the next Denver convention.

Cindy told us, upon retiring that first evening, that she and Josh were early risers. We were not to worry about getting up, but she would have coffee on and rolls out about 6:00 a.m. This would be my chance to see what people really do eat at that time of the morning. Since Bill and I were sleeping in the living room, adjacent to the kitchen and dining room, we had a worm's-eye view of this couple's early-morning relationship.

Early, early in the morning we heard the quiet sounds of someone working in the kitchen and then the murmur of voices and gentle clink of coffee cups. Josh and Cindy sat companionably at their kitchen table with their Bibles open. While reading, they would often stop and share with each other the richness of God's word, discussing it quietly. Eventually, as the rest of the household began to wake up, a tape of exuberant worship music came on, and the day began.

That evening, after a wonderfully prepared dinner, our families sat around the table and visited. We told stories, laughed at jokes, shared music and songs, played instruments, and talked about the Lord and His goodness to us all. The deep respect and love Josh and Cindy had for each other, their joy in sharing their home with others, and their single-hearted commitment to the Lord shone throughout the evening, making that spot a taste of heaven on earth. Perfection? No. Reality? Yes.

Our Journal

I don't know how it happened. We had always homeschooled, always had "Build one another up in love" as our family motto, always cared about developing good relationships within the family, but for some reason, Isaac and Melody could barely stand to be in the same room with each other. Apart, they were loving and kind, but put them together and WATCH OUT!

This attitude toward each other had been steadily growing for several years when we made our move to South Dakota. Going from a three-thousand-square-foot house to three small bedrooms did not promote peace between these two. Actually, the proximity dramatically increased hostility, and nothing we tried made any difference.

That was the situation when we decided to take our "show on the road," and become exhibitors at conventions in the Midwest. Though we jumped at the opportunity to sell these wonderful books to our favorite kind of people (you!), we did wonder what was going to happen when we stuffed all five of us, with all of our paraphernalia, into the minivan for weeks at a time. It was probably going to be a case of sink or swim, and we fervently prayed that the prognosis for our family was "swim!"

The children took turns having a bench seat all to themselves (the preferred spot), and sharing a seat with one sibling (the fighting spot). When it was time for Isaac and Melody to share the back seat, we prepared to enforce the Geneva Convention!

What developed over the next several weeks was very interesting. The moment bickering, fighting, unkindness, or sarcasm was heard, we put a stop to it. (There were several occasions when we stopped everything and pulled over to the side of the road to work this out.) We spent nearly every waking moment together: in the car, in restaurants, in motels. There was no one else to talk to but "us," there were no other friends but "us," there were no places to go where it wasn't filled with "us." It was a clear example of, "Wherever you go, there you are!" And that enforced togetherness, coupled with a firm adherence to the laws of love—"Speak the truth in love," "Let the law of kindness be in your mouth," "Build one another up in love," "Whatsoever things are true, noble, just, pure, lovely, of good report, virtuous or praiseworthy, think on these things" [and talk about them!]—began to produce an amazing result. Our children began to knit together, developing deeper friendships with one another, sharing their thoughts about the humors and rigors of traveling, creating on-the-spot games to play with one another, and caring about the other's needs.

Bill and I look back in awe and gratitude for what happened in our family that year. Isaac and Melody have become good friends. There is an air of friendliness pervading our home, replacing the former air of turmoil. Isaac, Michael, and Melody now spend time playfully teasing, laughing, sharing, and working peacefully together. Life in our home is much better than it used to be. Are our children perfect? No. Do they always get along? No. Do they ever argue? Yes. Do we ever have to remind them of the laws of love? Often. But that year they tasted the goodness of family friendship, and they have begun the process of building forever relationships with one another. It's a start! To paraphrase Zechariah 4:10, "Who despises the day of small beginnings?"

Are You Married to Your Best Friend?

This chapter is devoted to the concept that we, as members of a family, can develop lifelong "best" friendships with one another and that these friendships are of more value than gold. I have watched a number of homeschooling families around the nation who exhibit very special, wonderful relationships within the family, and I have pondered what priorities exist in their relationships to make them so special. The following are the elements we have seen in others and have experienced in our own family that make family friendships so strong and abiding. Remember, I am neither a family counselor nor a psychologist, but rather, I am a homeschool mom who has met lots of healthy families. Here are the things we've learned.

I once heard Josh McDowell say that the best thing a father can do for his children is to *love* his wife. The converse is also true, since it is the foundational love between husband and wife that provides a secure setting for children to grow. And committed, servant-style friendship is the real basis for a deep and abiding love between a married couple—enjoying each other's company, wanting to share what's important, learning to give as well as take, choosing the path that leads to the other's best.

Do significant, forever friendships just happen? Are they like colds—do you just come down with them one day? Or are they more like a rare treasure acquired through great effort, something to be cared for, nurtured, and protected? I believe that the latter is true, but how does one acquire this rare and precious treasure?

Cultivating a best-friend status with *anyone* requires certain elements:

⚬⚬⚬ Commitment—the foundation stone for friendship. If you cannot trust that I will be there in the bad times as well as the good, for better and for worse, in sickness and in health, our friendship will not last.

⚬⚬⚬ Unselfish, unconditional love. The best expression of this kind of love is found in 1 Corinthians 13. (It is God's *agapè* love.)

⚬⚬⚬ A servant's heart—willingness to cheerfully serve the other (this means from husband to wife and wife to husband, as well as parents to children and children to parents).

⚬⚬⚬ Respect—each for the other, expressed in attitude, words, and deeds.

⚬⚬⚬ Sensitivity—paying attention to the other's needs, learning when the other needs to be left alone or needs to talk.

⚬⚬⚬ Honesty—not the kind of "honesty" that angrily says, "I'm going to tell you just what I think!" but rather the honesty that carefully and lovingly tells the truth.

⚬⚬⚬ Vulnerability—making the choice to let someone know us as we really are, in the depth of our being.

⚬⚬⚬ Time—both in quantity and quality.

⚬⚬⚬ Effort—to be a good listener, to learn what matters to each other, to do what the other wants to do (even if it sometimes means fishing when you'd rather shop!).

ᴏᴍᴏ Humor—enjoying life together, seeing the humor and sharing it, choosing to encourage each other to look on the bright side in difficult times. ("After all, dear, if you hadn't dropped that cake on the floor, we'd have never had this wonderful apple pie from the bakery.")

If your relationship with your spouse is based on a growing, developing friendship, great! Be encouraged in the midst of homeschooling to still make time for the necessary ingredients of communication, laughter, sharing, and dreaming. If your relationship with your spouse is not thriving, I am deeply sorry! Without offering tired, worn-out clichés, consider long and hard the encouraging truth that our God is a *redeeming* God. He can "restore the years that the locusts have eaten" (Joel 2:25). He can truly, through His almighty power working within us, make our marriages better than they ever were before This is not normally an overnight transformation, but a "line upon line, here a little, there a little" kind of miracle. He is faithful.

Sometimes we become so busy in trying to hold our homeschools, our finances, our children, or our businesses together that we neglect to care for the primary human relationship, the marriage. At some point, we shake our heads and ask, "What's wrong with us?" Usually the problem can be traced back to a lack of time together: time *not* spent praying, talking, evaluating, planning, discussing, praying some more, relaxing, or laughing together.

Not spending enough time together is like removing the oil from a well-oiled machine. The friction caused from lack of oil on the moving parts will eventually cause the machine to break down. Evidently, then, we need to spend time together. What kind of time? Must it all be intense, businesslike, and work-oriented? I confess to having more than my share of "otter" in my makeup—otters are the funloving critters of the animal world—but it seems very important to the health of a relationship to spend at least *some* time relaxing, enjoying just being together (call it a date if you wish). Take walks in a beautiful location, laugh over the antics of a kitten, share a good book out loud, dream about delightful plans for the future, and eat a special candlelight dinner together, alone! (There have been times when, after we put our children to bed, we pulled out the china, candles, etc., and had a late-night romantic supper. If you haven't tried this, I highly recommend it.)

Time spent praying together and sharing God's word with each other is also a critical component in our friendship. One of the pastors from our church in Washington went suddenly from being burdened and depressed to cheerful and encouraged. I asked him what on earth happened, and he replied, "I've started praying with my wife every day. You can't imagine what a difference it is making in my life as we bring our burdens before the Lord, *together*." That was such an encouragement to us to *make* the time for prayer together, and over the years it has borne much fruit. As a current worship chorus says, "If just one of us can put a thousand to flight, then two of us can send the legions fleeing."

We also need time together to evaluate and make plans for home-schooling. Sharing the concerns, the successes, the dreams, and the needs makes it so much easier! It's like the oxen or draft horses who were yoked together for work—two pulling on that plow are better than one. So we also need to be yoked together in our family work—two heads are much better than one. And it is amazing how, when the homeschooling mom is absolutely stymied over something, the dad, with a different view-point, is often able to make a simple suggestion that solves the problem.

Do you remember my story about feeling overwhelmed by my "police" duties (with chores, clean-up, etc.)? When, after coming to the point of wanting to give up homeschooling completely, I finally brought this burden to Bill, he helped me through it. This partnership has worked very well for us, especially since I no longer feel as if I am respon-sible for the whole ball of wax. We are partners, in life, in homeschool, in the family unit.

Time together, if it is to be realistic, also includes the times of diffi-culties. There are those moments in our lives when things are not at all the way we planned, unforeseen difficulties emerge, or tragedy strikes. Bill and I have found as we weather the storm together—praying, shar-ing, encouraging each other—that our relationship has grown deeper. James 1:2–4 (Amplified Bible) says, "Consider it wholly joyful, my brethren, whenever you are enveloped in or encounter trials of any sort, or fall into various temptations. Be assured and understand that the trial and proving of your faith bring out endurance and steadfastness and patience. But let endurance and steadfastness and patience have full play and do a thorough work, so that you may be perfectly and fully devel-oped, lacking nothing." Amen. Go on through the trial together then, and wait for that good end.

If we picture our marriage relationship as an incredibly special, beautiful flower, we would have to say that some of us have orchids, oth-ers have gardenias, still others have old-fashioned roses, and perhaps some even have dinner-plate dahlias. Each of these flowers has some needs in common (soil, water, sun), but they all also have needs peculiar to themselves. It is the same with us! We all need the basics (as outlined in the list at the beginning of the chapter of elements for cultivating a best-friend status), but beyond that, our relationships need whatever else is peculiar to each of us and our situation. If you live fifty miles from your nearest neighbor, you may occasionally *need* to be with other families. If you live on a family compound with thousands of aunt, uncles, cousins, and visitors, you may occasionally *need* to get away. If your family lives in the northwoods of Minnesota, you may feel an urge to visit a city. If you live in Manhattan, you may feel an urge to visit the pristine wilderness. As you and your spouse learn to care for the special needs of the other, your forever friendship will grow. May God make our marriages flowering plants that go deep into the earth while reaching high into the heavens, producing bountiful, fragrant harvests.

Parents and Children in Friendship

Though we don't watch television shows, friends have told us about the many, many sitcoms that portray parents as stupid and their children as cool. The kids constantly put their parents down, and the parents yell, ineffectively, at these homegrown monsters, or they try a little pop psychology on them, which is also ineffective.

Many parents choose to homeschool their children to counter this trend for their own family. They work hard and sacrifice much to build a different kind of relationship. And if the sampling of homeschooling families we've seen gives any indication, it's working! Parents and children are not only co-existing peacefully but also enjoying one another.

One day, in reading an Edith Schaeffer book, I came across an amazing idea. The author described her husband and her children as her best friends, saying that she would rather be with them than with anyone else. My husband was already my best friend, but my children? That took some thinking. The perception of my children in my mind was that they were infinitely precious and loved, and I had a definite responsibility to nurture and raise them properly. But for them to become my best friends, some things were going to have to change.

All the areas of cultivating a best friend (listed earlier in the chapter) had to be fleshed out anew in reference to my children:

- ⌒ commitment
- ⌒ unselfish, unconditional love

- ᥅ a servant's heart
- ᥅ respect
- ᥅ sensitivity
- ᥅ honesty
- ᥅ vulnerability
- ᥅ time
- ᥅ effort
- ᥅ humor

Looking at the list, I realized that such a friendship definitely required a commitment as well as unselfish, unconditional love. Much of our experiences in parenting included being a servant to our children's needs, and as homeschoolers we were certainly spending quantity time with our children. But how about the areas of respect, sensitivity, honesty, vulnerability, effort (to be a good listener, etc.), and humor? In all honesty, some of these ideas were not uppermost in my mind as I related to my children. It had seemed enough to simply love them, feed them, teach them, clothe them, shop for them, and read to them. But under the gentle prompting of the Holy Spirit, things began to change.

I saw the need to give them the same type of respect that I was expecting them to give me. If I expected them to not interrupt me, then I should not interrupt them. If speaking in a respectful manner was the rule for the children, then Mom needed to speak to them respectfully as well (even when bringing correction!). If they were expected to respect our belongings, then we needed to respect theirs as well (even if it meant not throwing away an eyesore of a "craft" that held special place in their heart). The point is (and it is certainly a biblical principle), "Do unto others as you would have them do unto you." [Diana's maxim: What's good for the goose is good for the goslings!]

When it came to sensitivity, my scorecard was 1–1. There were times when I understood what my children were feeling, when they needed to talk, when we would cancel everything else to air their thoughts. But other times, I was so immersed in my own thing that I had no regard for my children's needs. (At times my family would describe me as driven!) Again, the Holy Spirit brought correction to my heart. I had to ask my children for forgiveness, and we had a very special time of being honest with one another. They now have my express permission to "get in my face" if I am not paying attention to their needs.

In the areas of honesty and vulnerability, we are learning how to communicate. One evening at the dinner table, Isaac made a joke that backfired. His words insulted me, though he had not realized the import of what he had said. We excused ourselves from the table immediately to work this conflict out. I was furious with him and privately told him so. As we continued to dialogue, I suddenly remembered an incident from my own childhood when I had insulted a guest in our home, though it was completely unintentional. I had had no clue that the words were offensive. My parents had made me to understand, in no uncertain terms, that my mistake was *never* to be repeated. As Isaac and I laughed over my memory, I realized that his was an honest mistake (no offense intended), and he realized how important it is to be aware of our words. He was genuinely sorry for what he had said, and I was genuinely sorry for getting angry over a mistake. We asked forgiveness of each other, hugged, and went back to the table to resume our dinner. God grant us the wisdom to be honest and vulnerable with our children, admitting our own foibles as we struggle to raise them up in the "fear and admonition of the Lord."

"Do you hear what I hear?" Listening is an art, as we all know, but *making time* to listen is a discipline, and it takes effort. We must make a choice whether or not to stop what we're doing, look at our child, and focus our concentration on what is being said. Have you ever been reading the newspaper and had one of your children start up a conversation? "Hey, Mom, guess what? We just read the neatest thing in the encyclopedia about the Komodo dragon." You just grunt affirmatively from time to time as the child continues to wax eloquent. When the "conversation" is over and the child has skipped off to the kitchen, you wonder, "What? Did I just agree to purchasing tickets to the island of Komodo?!" Maybe this doesn't describe you, but it hits very close to home for me. (At the same time, it is important to teach our children that it is polite to ask permission before they interrupt our reading. That way we have a chance to stop and listen.) It has become evident that to really listen to our child (or our husband, or our neighbor), we need to stop what we are doing (unless you honestly can work with your hands and listen to what is being said) and focus on that person. It is neither natural nor easy for many of us, but it's worth it when we hear what our children are saying. And guess what? Since we reap what we sow, perhaps, if we sow listening ears, we will reap children who listen! [Diana's maxim: You get what you listen for.]

Humor, I believe, doesn't just happen, it must be cultivated and appreciated. As God started working in my heart in this area, I realized that much of the time I was entirely too uptight with my children, demanding perfection of them constantly—especially during meals. When we began to relax a little bit and laugh at the funny things being said at the dinner table, everyone heaved a big sigh of relief. It is amazing how many funny stories from our childhood we never told our children before, but now that humor has become a priority for us, we often sit around the table and "let 'er rip!" Every one of us knows the rules of etiquette and propriety, but there are times when, for the sake of forever friendship, we need to break loose and *laugh* with one another.

One source of constant amusement in our home is our dogs, Max and Miggie. Max is a beagle/basset cross that was once described by the vet as "two dogs long and half a dog high." Miggie is our indefatigable dachshund with an attitude. The dogs keep us in continuous giggles as they moan piteously over food, eat jealously from the other's dish, act as slow-moving sundials (changing their position on the rug according to the sunlight), and play determinedly with each other (Bark. Jump. Bark. Jump. Bark. Run. Bark). Their antics are something we point out to one another, sharing humor across generational lines. If humor is lacking in your home, consider getting a pet with personality. It will more than repay in mirth what you spend on pet food.

We also need to spend quality time with our children, like the dates with our spouses. For friendship to grow, we need to have enjoyable moments with one another, not just "make your bed, do your math, clear the table, go to bed" moments, but listening moments, sharing-a-dream moments, special experience moments, moments that build memories and companionship.

One time we had the opportunity to visit Niagara Falls in New York state. We had heard people say, "It's no big deal, not worth the trouble," but we wanted to see for ourselves. As we walked down the path to Horseshoe Falls, the sound of a continuous, mighty roar resounded. We saw billowing clouds rise up from a distance, and then, finally, there were the magnificent falls themselves. As we stood on the edge of the falls, looking at one of the most awesome, breath-taking sights in the world, something wonderful was indelibly written on our memories. It was a shared moment of magnificence, an experience never to be forgotten by any of us. Such moments and memories are important in the building of forever friendships with our children, whether they take place across the nation or across the living room. How good it will be to one day hear our children say (or sing) to us: "Thanks for the memories..."

Brotherly (and Sisterly) Love

Having been an only child, I do not personally understand the dynamics of sibling rivalry. It always seemed to me that it would be the greatest thing in the world to have brothers and sisters. But after the second child, Michael, was born into my little family, I received a crash course on this phenomenon. With the addition of Melody, we were into full-blown sibling rivalry.

Not knowing that this was "normal," "nothing to worry about," "something to ignore," "something they'll grow out of," we felt our only sensible recourse was to let the Scriptures be our guide. 1 John 4:20 and 21 states, "If someone says, 'I love God,' and hates his brother, he is a liar; for he who does not love his brother whom he has seen, how can he love God whom he has not seen? And this commandment we have from Him: that he who loves God *must* love his brother also." I—the naive, optimistic, only child, who doesn't know the reality of sibling rivalry—did not say this; God said it! And if it's true for the Church, how much more should it be true for the family?

How, then, do we encourage this love between brothers and sisters in a family? How do we help our children cultivate a forever friend status with one another? What steps can be taken to foster harmony and love?

The first step, I believe, is to voice the expectation: "You will *always* be brothers and sisters! Other friends will come and go, but apart from the person you marry, your brothers and sisters have the most staying power of any relationships you'll ever have. Therefore, be wise about this natural resource and build a lifelong friendship with each other." Granted, you may have to say this more than once(!); in fact, you may have to write it on all the walls of the house. But when it starts to sink in, this expectation will have a definite effect on relationships.

Isaac and Michael are two very different young men. Isaac is an extrovert, enjoying talking to a million people at once, the life of the party. Michael is an introvert, a thinker, a mull-things-over-before-you-speak kind of guy. He enjoys one-on-one discussions, hiking with a friend, and solitude. When Isaac and Michael run into the inevitable problems of living and communicating with an opposite, we remind them of God's wisdom in selecting them as brothers and life-long relatives. In fact, we point out that God is probably preparing them for life by giving them each someone who is hard to get along with as a roommate. The brothers usually grimace, then grin, then laugh at the possibility.

We need to teach our children the same rules of friendship previously listed: commitment, unselfish, unconditional love, a servant's heart, respect, sensitivity, honesty, vulnerability, time, effort, and humor. As they learn that these are the tools, the means, the methods of building friendships, our children will be more aware of just exactly what it takes to develop a good relationship with the person they're sharing a room with. They need to understand that we don't save our company behavior just for company, but we extend the same courtesy, politeness, thoughtfulness, and kindness to one another on a daily basis. (Remember, "It is not what's taught, but what's caught that counts!" It starts with Dad and Mom, then parents to children, and finally comes out in sibling relationships.)

Though Michael and Melody usually get along famously, there are moments when we hear them caterwauling. Often the problem turns out to be a simple miscommunication, but because they did not listen to each other, did not show common courtesy, did not give the benefit of the doubt, an argument erupted. We are encouraged, however, because as they are learning how to deal with misunderstandings in a more mature manner, the decibel level has decreased dramatically.

Does this happen automatically? Is it natural? Is it normal? No. But it *is* possible, especially for homeschoolers, since we are always around to help remind the siblings of the rule "Build one another up in love." And just as they slowly but surely learn to read, write, use a napkin, make their bed, etc., they will also learn to respect, serve, love, and laugh with one another in a loving, godly way.

We also need to be aware of the dynamics of relationships outside the family that may be destructive to relationships within the family. It is important to watch for outside friendships that mock or taunt younger siblings, resulting in an attitude in our own children. This is not to say that our children shouldn't have wonderful friendships with many people outside the family, but we need to be aware of which friendships are sabotaging sibling relationships. If we see that happening, we must take whatever steps are necessary to stop the destruction. We keep emphasizing to our children the specialness and uniqueness of their relationship with one another and try to protect that budding friendship from being squashed by those who are not motivated by Hebrews 13:1, "Let brotherly love continue." It may limit your child's "social calendar," but it will certainly deepen and enrich the true friendships your child does have.

One of the reasons brotherly love may not seem realistic to us is that in our culture we have no role models for brothers and sisters caring for each other. Therefore we have no expectation that it is possible. If we do not think such a thing is possible, we will not hold up a standard of kindness and love in our families. And remember, if we do not have a goal to aim for, we will surely miss it.

Be encouraged. With God, "all things are possible." Our families and homes can be a safe haven rather than a battlefield. We can grow together instead of apart. We can know the richness God intended for the family rather than the desolation and hopelessness of our culture's solution. Exerting the effort to cultivate healthy relationships while we are continuing to provide thoughtful, careful homeschooling will bring the *abundant* homeschool lifestyle. The promised land is, in fact, a reality!

Epilogue

*T*hank you for allowing us to share a bit of our journey with you. It has been a journey of laughter and of tears, remembering mostly the joys but also the realities of the trek. I pray that this glimpse into our family, along with those things we have learned from other "settlers," will encourage you and make a difference in your commitment to continue. If you have been encouraged, inspired, or enlightened, the effort of communicating will have been worthwhile.

Heading off to the Promised Land of Abundant Homeschooling may seem a little daunting at first. You will, as did every other traveler before you, encounter some difficulties on the journey. There may be days when you wish you had never started in the first place, but rest assured, those days will pass. After crossing through the Desert of Not-Knowing-How and climbing over the Mountain Ranges of Resistance, Failure, and Weariness, you will find yourself in a land "flowing with milk and honey."

The seeds of loving family relationships and interesting education that you faithfully plant *will* produce fruit, but remember that a harvest takes time. Your children will experience what it is to be healthy in relationship and to be curious and hungry to know about learning. They will know the joys of friendly discussion, hilarious laughter, and creative artistry, all within the safe haven of your home. You will all learn what it is to serve the needs of the other and that others in your family think differently than you do, which will result in an understanding, compassionate attitude. You will make memories together, forge friendships, work side by side, and enjoy the bounty of God's abundance.

Dear brothers and sisters, if you have read this book wistfully, wishing "if only" this could be true, be encouraged. We have seen many, many families around the nation experiencing this good and fruitful promised land in their own homes. The goal is neither impossible nor unattainable. The delight of living an abundant homeschooling lifestyle can be much more than pie in the sky—it can be a life-changing reality. It will develop in time through commitment and humor, grace and forgiveness, wisdom and humility, discipline and freedom, listening and sharing, compassion and mercy, accomplished in the daily strength of our Lord.

"My strength is made perfect in weakness" (2 Corinthians 12:9).

DIANA WARING, a graduate of Western Washington University in Bellingham, Washington, has been homeschooling for ten years. She is also a musician, composer, playwright, seminar and retreat speaker, and author of *History Alive! Through Music: America, History Alive! Through Music: Westward Ho!* and of *Beyond Survival: A Guide to Abundant-Life Homeschooling.* Her seminars of history on cassette, *What in the World's Going on Here? Volume 1 and Volume 2* and *History Via the Scenic Route: Getting off the Textbook Interstate,* are used by such diverse groups as history professors and homeschooling children. The homespun concert of American history in folk music "Yankee Doodle Tells a Tale" has been performed across the nation by Diana and her family to the enthusiastic delight of young and old alike.

Diana brings encouragement, instruction and laughter wherever she speaks. For the past several years, she has traveled extensively with her husband and three children, speaking to audiences from coast to coast.

For information regarding booking Diana as a seminar, retreat or convention speaker or for booking the concert "Yankee Doodle Tells a Tale," please write:

Diana Waring
c/o Emerald Books
P.O. Box 635
Lynnwood, Washington 98046

*"**S**ince this is a new way of studying history which many of us have not experienced, I highly recommend to you Diana Waring's tape series,* **What in the World's Going on Here?...**

"Diana teaches us how to re-evaluate world history from an eternal perspective: God sovereignly ruling over the affairs of men and nations."

CATHY DUFFY

" **...A**n outstanding Judeo-Christian primer of world history. Discover Jesus Christ as the centerpiece of all human history."*

BUILDER BOOKS

What in the World - vol. 1

"Have you wondered where the Bible fits into ancient civilizations, or how the history of the Church impacts world history? Enjoy Diana Waring's animated presentation in this extraordinary adventure through world history - from Creation to the French Revolution."

History Via the Scenic Route:

"Diana Waring's second series teaches you how to make history your child's favorite subject. A fabulous how-to resource for do-it-yourself unit studies using literature, art, music, math, science, even cooking! Refreshing, practical and inspirational - the enthusiasm is contagious!"

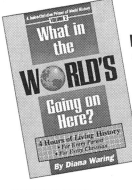

What in the World - vol. 2

"Did the missions movement change world history? Was prayer the underlying reason behind Hitler's mistakes? Join Diana Waring for this amazing look at history from the time of Napoleon to the rebirth of Israel as a nation."

Available Through:

Emerald Books
P.O. Box 635
Lynnwood, WA 98046
VISA/MC orders only call 1-800-922-2143